PERSUADE US TO REJOICE

Also by Robert McAfee Brown

Spirituality and Liberation: Overcoming the Great Fallacy

Religion and Violence (Second Edition)

Saying Yes and Saying No: On Rendering to God and Caesar

The Bible Speaks to You

Unexpected News: Reading the Bible with Third World Eyes

Making Peace in the Global Village

Theology in a New Key: Responding to Liberation Themes

The Significance of the Church

THE LIBERATING POWER OF FICTION

PERSUADE US TO REJOICE

Robert McAfee Brown

WESTMINSTER/JOHN KNOX PRESS
Louisville, Kentucky

Scripture quotations marked RSV are from the Revised Standard Version of the Bible, copyrighted 1946, 1952, © 1971, 1973 by the Division of Christian Education of the National Council of the Churches of Christ in the U.S.A. and are used by permission.

Scripture quotations marked NRSV are from the New Revised Standard Version of the Bible, copyrighted © 1989 by the Division of Christian Education of the National Council of the Churches of Christ in the U.S.A. and are used by permission.

Scripture quotations marked NEB are taken from *The New English Bible,* © The Delegates of the Oxford University Press and The Syndics of the Cambridge University Press, 1961, 1970. Used by permission.

Scripture quotations marked REB are taken from *The Revised English Bible,* © Oxford University Press and Cambridge University Press, 1989. Used by permission.

Copyright acknowledgments are found on page 8.

Book design by Publishers' WorkGroup

First edition

Published by Westminster/John Knox Press
Louisville, Kentucky

This book is printed on acid-free paper that meets the American National Standards Institute Z39.48 standard. ∞

PRINTED IN THE UNITED STATES OF AMERICA

9 8 7 6 5 4 3 2 1

Library of Congress Cataloging-in-Publication Data

Brown, Robert McAfee, 1920–
    Persuade us to rejoice : the liberating power of fiction / Robert McAfee Brown. — 1st ed.
        p.   cm.
    Includes bibliographical references.
    ISBN 0-664-25381-4 (alk. paper)

    1. Fiction—Religious aspects—Christianity.   2. Faith in literature.   3. Religion and literature.   4. Fiction—History and criticism.   I. Title.
PN3351.B76   1992
809.3'9382—dc20   91-45743

Follow, poet, follow right
To the bottom of the night,
With your unconstraining voice
Still persuade us to rejoice;

With the farming of a verse
Make a vineyard of the curse,
Sing of human unsuccess
In a rapture of distress;

In the deserts of the heart
Let the healing fountain start,
In the prison of his days
Teach the free man how to praise.

—W. H. Auden,
"In Memory of W. B. Yeats"

CONTENTS

IV

ACKNOWLEDGMENTS

Grateful acknowledgment is made to the following for permission to reprint the following copyrighted material:

To *Christianity and Crisis* for slightly adapted versions of the following: "Alan Paton" (June 6, 1988); "The Fall and the Faith" (September 30, 1957); "The Land of the Blessed" (May 22, 1989); "Wonders of Music and Love" (May 6, 1986); and "Middle Earth and the People of Kesh" (May 19, 1987).

To *The Christian Century,* for "Elie Wiesel: Writer as Peacemaker." Copyright 1986 Christian Century Foundation. Adapted and reprinted by permission from the November 5, 1986, issue of *The Christian Century.*

To New York University Press, for "*Twilight*: Madness, Caprice, Friendship, and God," in Rittner, ed., *Elie Wiesel: Between Memory and Hope* (1990). Reprinted by permission of New York University Press.

To *Religion and Literature,* for "The Nathan Syndrome: Stories with a Moral Intention" (Winter 1984). Reprint permission granted by *Religion and Literature,* University of Notre Dame, Notre Dame, IN 46556.

To Mme. Darina Silone, for quotations from Ignazio Silone, *Bread and Wine* and *Fontamara* (New York: New American Library, Signet Classic, 1986), trans. Eric Mosbacher. Translations for both works are copyright © 1986 Darina Silone.

To *Theology Today,* for "Charles Williams: Lay Theologian" (July 1953). Adapted and reprinted by permission of *Theology Today.*

To the University of Pittsburgh Press, for "Ignazio Silone and the Pseudonyms of God," in *The Shapeless God: Essays on Modern Fiction,* Harry J. Mooney and Thomas F. Staley, editors. Published in 1968 by the University of Pittsburgh Press. This revision reprinted by permission of the publisher.

To Random House for material excerpted from the following:
Ani Maamin: A Song Lost and Found Again, by Elie Wiesel. Copyright © 1973 by Elie Wiesel. Reprinted by permission of Random House, Inc.

"Brother to Dragons," by Robert Penn Warren. Copyright © 1953 by Robert Penn Warren. Reprinted by permission of Random House, Inc.

"In Memory of W. B. Yeats," in *W. H. Auden: Collected Poems,* by W. H. Auden, ed. by Edward Mendelson. Copyright 1940 and renewed 1968 by W. H. Auden. Reprinted by permission of Random House, Inc.

INTRODUCTION
"Persuade Us to Rejoice"

In a story called "Leaf by Niggle," J. R. R. Tolkien acquaints us with a fussy little man whose obsession in life is to finish painting a landscape that has come to be dominated by a huge tree. For a variety of reasons—his inability to say no to the incessant demands of his neighbor Parrish, and an ongoing feeling that with just a little more work the painting could be even better—the picture is never completed.

After his death, Niggle finds himself in a strange land, and after various adventures he begins to notice items here and there in the landscape that are vaguely familiar; has he, indeed, been here before? At one point in his wanderings he looks up and is astonished—so astonished that he falls off his bicycle. For there, facing him, in all the fullness of its three-dimensional glory, is *his tree*—finished just as he had imagined countless times it would be one day, if ever he had the time for it and was not distracted by outside pressures. He is inside his own picture.

> He gazed at the Tree, and slowly he lifted up his arms and opened them wide.
> "It's a gift!" he said. He was referring to his art, and also to the results; but he was using the word quite literally.

The presence of the finished tree "persuades [him] to rejoice."

Reasons to "rejoice" are hard to come by these days. All of us have private and public lists of woes that continually threaten to consign joy, laughter, rejoicing, and praise to the scrap heap. In a world of savage wars, homelessness, drugs, death camps, refugees, unemployment, infant mortality, and nationalistic chauvinism, a summons to "rejoice" seems unrealistic if not uncaring.

And yet the summons is issued. It is issued (as the W. H. Auden epigraph reminds us) from the world of artistic sensibility. And it is issued (as frequent exhortations to "rejoice, give thanks, and sing" remind us) from the world of religious sensibility as well. The poet, Auden reminds us, must risk being honest about our plight, going "to the *bottom* of the night," where things are bleakest, likening our situation to that of a prison. No false sentimentalism here. And it is in the midst of just such deprivation that the poet must "still persuade us to rejoice." It is a tall order. Auden insists that no matter what our situation, both the call to rejoice and the call to praise are valid. (That these lines are being written in the waiting room of a dentist's office is only the smallest vindication of Auden's existential persuasiveness.)

One need not be "religious" to engage in rejoicing, though I think it helps. But we must not be too dogmatic in advancing such a claim. When Niggle lifts his arms, opens them wide, and says, exultantly, "It's a gift!" he is not in any explicit way rejoicing in God. At least, however, he is rejoicing

> . . . in the beauty in which he is now enfolded;
> . . . in his awareness of this enfolding;
> . . . in the realization that he has been allowed to contribute to the fullness of the present moment;
> . . . in the recognition that a portion of his life, hitherto fragmented and interrupted, has come to fruition;
> . . . in the sheer wonder that all of the above can happen, and that the universe is so constructed that meaning, rather than chaos, appears to characterize it;
> . . . in the fact that he does not have to piece all this together by himself but can be content to notice that it *has* been pieced together.

In sum, he is rejoicing over what he could not have anticipated, since it was not an attainment but, as he precisely acknowledges, "a gift."

Such a response yields an attitude that can, in my lexicon at least, be characterized as "religious"—full of wonder, joy, gratitude, unexpectedness, rejoicing—though I shall not prematurely baptize those who prefer to exempt themselves from the characterization.

In any event, there is a promising by-product of the rejoicing. *It draws us all together:*

A shepherd alone on a hillside, searching all night for a lost sheep, finds it, "and home he goes to call his friends and neighbours together. 'Rejoice with me!' he cries. 'I have found my lost sheep' " (Luke 15:6, NEB). A widow who loses a coin looks everywhere until she finds it, "and when she has, she calls her friends and neighbours together, and says, 'Rejoice with me! I have found the piece that I lost' " (Luke 15:9, NEB).

Once Niggle has realized that he is to engage in ongoing three-dimensional landscaping, he reflects, "Of course. . . . What I need is Parrish," and the two of them combine their different skills to create fresh beauty.

Two people fall in love and the cause for rejoicing is so great that they seek out friends with whom to share the good news.

Hymns of rejoicing capture the same communal impulse; rejoicing is to be shared between "bright youth and snow-crowned age."

Everyone is to join in the dance.

If that seems too benign a rendering of life's possibilities, let us at least entertain it for the moment.

The subtitle reads, "The Liberating Power of Fiction." Limiting the material for examination to "fiction" (with a couple of exceptions that will be readily apparent to the reader) is an arbitrary device to keep the volume from becoming too hefty. The relation of fiction to faith will have transfer value to other art forms, such as sculpture, drama, graphics, photography, music, painting, and working with fabrics or anodized aluminum. But we must ask others to make such connections; the space available here is already over booked.

By "fiction" we will mean literary creations in which the characters "exist" only in the author's head and yet confront us as "real people" to whom we can relate and by whom we can be challenged or sustained. If the writer is a good writer, the human situation depicted will not only illumine the specific time and place the characters inhabit but will offer perspectives on struggles in which many of us participate as we try to distinguish between good and evil, between competing values and choices, those things that are the stuff of human quests and quandaries.

It is precisely this characteristic that makes it possible to describe our immersion in fiction as "liberating." For fiction confronts us with possibilities for our own lives that might have remained forever hidden, if the authors had not described the choices open to their own characters, in ways that opened new vistas for us as well. We see how Robinson Crusoe deals with abandonment, how Huckleberry Finn deals with racism, or how Harriet Vane deals with the likelihood of a "guilty" verdict in her own murder trial, and we cannot avoid asking ourselves how we would react in similar situations. We become better acquainted with who we actually are, and we can sometimes be liberated to understand ourselves in new ways, drawing on resources we did not previously realize were available to us.

"Liberation" is, of course, a big word in theology these days. While it refers, as it always has, to liberation from the corrosive power of sin and guilt, its particular contemporary contribution is to highlight the additional possibilities of liberation from the power of (a) oppressive social structures, and (b) the grip of impersonal "fate," both of which initially suggest that we can do nothing to bring about change. Exploration of these new possibilities can be aided by the fiction we read, and the ongoing possibility of a greater measure of liberation is surely one of the things most calculated to "persuade us to rejoice." We are not enmeshed in wrongdoing so deeply that escape is impossible; we are not doomed to be crushed by the impersonal forces of a market economy, nor are we caught in an ineluctable web of fate.

These concerns for liberation from inner dislocation, societal destructiveness, and fatal entrapment are concerns not only of theologians but of novelists as well, and the two disciplines working in tandem can offer occasions for us to participate in fiction's liberating power.

There is a final thing to be said: this book is a modest attempt to hedge my bets with mortality. For years I have been trying (with a frustrating lack of success) to reshape a sizable mountain of notes into a book on "theology as narrative." Whether or not I will ever complete this daunting project is one of my life's unresolved mysteries. If I do not, I want at least to have left this small token of gratitude to the authors treated here—not only those who happen to be Christians, but also those whom Friedrich Schleiermacher called "religion's cultured despisers." (It is instructive to me that in the pages that follow, the latter outnumber the former about two to one.) My increasing personal debt to women authors only begins to receive acknowledgment in these pages, and one strong motivation for completing the larger work is to illustrate the scope of that indebtedness.

The structure of the book is simple. The three initial chapters raise overall questions about relating faith and fiction; each of the three middle chapters explores a single author through a variety of works from the available corpus in order to illustrate a variety of approaches; the seven final (and shorter) chapters react to individual books in order to render the discussion more specific. The Epilogue attempts to illustrate how each author has persuaded me to rejoice and invites readers who have hung in all the way to engage in a similar exercise.

I am indebted to Ursula LeGuin for many things, but particularly in this instance for her summary of Auden's theme (cited at the beginning of the Epilogue), which initially sparked the concerns of the book as a whole; to Judy Dunbar, who not only traced the theme back to Auden, but gave extraordinarily wise, critical, and creative counsel as the book was taking shape; and to Vivian Lindermayer, of the staff of *Christianity and Crisis,* for editorial help when some of the chapters were initially being prepared for publication in that journal. A fourth person deserves special comment. In the course of publishing fourteen books with Westminster Press, I could never give public thanks to Paul Meacham, the religion editor, who read and commented to me on the possibilities and the shortcomings of all those books, since the policy of the Press forbade mention in prefaces of its employees. But Paul Meacham has now retired, and so I am at liberty to thank him publicly for reading this manuscript and making numerous suggestions, threatening initially but creative finally, so that whatever merit the finished text has is largely due to him, while its still-present deficiencies will almost surely be those places where I ignored his good counsel. All four of the above friends and mentors are exonerated from responsibility for the finished product.

Finally, as always, thanks to Sydney, who knows that when I get a certain look in my eye a book is gestating, and that domestic schedules will be subject to upheaval until birth takes place. That despite such frequent intrusions she still loves me, is what most of all persuades me to rejoice.

Robert McAfee Brown

Palo Alto, California
Good Friday–Easter, 1991

I

1

THE POWER OF A STORY
The Nathan Syndrome

We approach any work of literature with suspicion if we think the writer is trying to make a moral point. We are afraid the evidence will be doctored, the cards stacked, the material (and ourselves) manipulated.

On the other hand, it is hard to conceive of a work of literature that does not have some kind of moral intention behind it. Surely a main reason for writing is that authors feel too strongly about something *not* to write, and they use fiction, drama, fantasy, myth, or the sonnet form to give expression to something in which they believe deeply. This can extend to many other art forms as well. Picasso's *Guernica* contains a passionate moral message and is nonetheless art because of it. The same can be said of the Vietnam War Memorial in Washington. Even Charles Schulz is not above communicating deep truths about human nature through his cartoon strip (never trust Lucy with a football at kickoff time). Indeed, if an author decided to write a novel that was deliberately designed to be devoid of moral content, that in itself would be a statement by the author about where moral content stood in his or her list of values, and thus a statement with a moral content of its own.

So perhaps the difficulty we feel when morality intrudes into a story too obviously is not a matter of authorial intentionality but of *flawed* intentionality. We feel that the author is cheating us when he or she has a "point" to make and simply manipulates a situation and a cast of characters to make the point in a contrived way. The characters are subordinated to the theme; they are so two-dimensional and fake as to be nothing more than vehicles to give the author a mouthpiece. They remain puppets in the hands of their creator, never assuming enough independent reality to go in directions that might complicate the point the author wants to make through them. (Steinbeck's *East of Eden*, to which reference will be made in the next chapter, veers in this direction.)

The *quality* of literature is crucial in determining how successfully the writer's moral vision is communicated to us. It must be an attractive temptation for an author describing a catastrophe to play on the reader's emotions, vulnerability, and voyeuristic impulses, spinning out the scenes in such a way that the reader is spared nothing. And yet when Elie Wiesel writes about Holocaust survivors, he communicates powerfully to readers who have had no direct experience of the Holocaust, precisely by an economy of words and images that result from intense discipline and an unwillingness to stoop to sensationalism. When one remembers that Wiesel's *Night, Dawn*, and *The Accident* all, in their paperback editions, have fewer than a hundred pages each, one realizes how successfully he has avoided the temptation to exploit his subject matter by extensive manipulation of the emotions of his readers. Instead of confronting a contrived appeal to horror, we confront a view of reality that enables us to engage with the story, because we trust the way the author's integrity is communicated through mastery of his craft.

This, it seems to me, is how we must approach literature that seeks to instruct, to inform, to challenge, to condemn, to liberate. Its importance to us is that on some level it "touches" us. However different the story on the lap of the reader is from the story going on in his or her life, if the reader can trust the author, the two stories will meet at some point and the reader's own life story will be up for reexamination. Whenever this happens, the stuff of a moral decision is being created. A dialectic results: if it is true that what *I bring* to the reading influences what I hear and how I respond, it is also true that the story *brings something to me* about which I have to make a judgment. The story might be set in the midst of a battle and trace the horrors of modern warfare. And through the mix of authorial vision and reader engagement, reading such a text could do a number of things to me: it might persuade me to become a pacifist; it might reinforce a feeling that a policy of "nuclear deterrence" is the only way to avoid war in the future; it might leave me in utter despair, convinced that there is nothing we can do about the state of the world; or it might trigger a conversion experience as a result of which I decide that only religion can save us.

The Power of the Story Then

Whatever the mix, and for whatever reasons, *stories have the potential to transform*, for good or ill. On the basis of that conviction I want to offer an example from the Hebrew scriptures of what happens when a story is explicitly told to produce moral change. Part of its strength lies in the fact that there is more than one way to read it, so that both writer and reader must struggle to arrive at authentic moral decisions. The story is not strictly "fiction" (save to those who choose to believe that the entire Bible is a misdirected exercise in make-believe), but we can surely claim that if the story had never happened, someone would have had to invent it.

It should be acknowledged in advance that biblical writers tend to be more didactic than contemporary writers, and that one reason they are didactic is that they give greater credence to a moral structure at the heart of things than is widespread among contemporary writers. However, if we bear these differences in mind, the degree to which a biblical story can still speak to our own age across the gap of centuries and worldviews will be even more remarkable.

The story we will examine describes a confrontation between a king (David) and a prophet (Nathan) and shows how "a story within the story" changes everything (2 Sam. 11–21). We might call it "The Nathan Syndrome."*

It is first of all the story of *David* and his adulterous relationship with Bathsheba—which is the way most comfortably situated people read it. To them it is a message of judgment, indicating that adultery is wrong and that its consequences lead to things like deception and murder. But it is also the story of *Nathan* and his stern relationship with David—which is the way most oppressed people suffering under evil tyrants read it. To them it is a message of hope, telling them that it is possible to stand up against those who abuse power and say no. Third, it is the story of *a ewe lamb*—an apparently innocent little fable that ties the stories of David and Nathan together in a definitive way. Let us examine them.

"The David Story" is a highly moral tale of the private and public consequences of personal iniquity. Although the language of most of our translations is a bit coy, it doesn't take much imagination to get behind it.

King David is at home in the palace while the troops are off in the hills doing battle. One afternoon he sees a woman, Bathsheba, sunbathing in the

---

*Here I must render an apology in advance: the next five or six pages have been lifted, almost without change, from another book. Before the currently widespread charge of "plagiarism" is laid at my doorstep, I should point out that I wrote the other book, called *Unexpected News*. Even so, it is considered Very Bad Form to put in a later book material that has already appeared in an earlier one. Readers tend to feel shortchanged when thus victimized. In extenuation of my departure from such authorial amenities, I can only plead that (a) the material thus pirated is right on target for illustrating the point of the entire chapter; (b) I worked very hard to create the original version and still find it readable and even a bit racy; and (c) not one reader in a thousand will have read it in its earlier appearance anyway.

nude and wants to have sex with her. A predictable two-step regal sequence follows: (1) king desires woman; (2) king gets woman. Only this time there is a third step: king gets woman . . . pregnant.

What to do? To complicate matters, the woman has a husband, Uriah. To complicate matters further, he is off with the troops in the army, loyally fighting the Ammonites for the king. David, who puts great stock in appearances, cooks up a scheme. Out of his great thoughtfulness for the needs of his fighting men, he will recall Uriah from the front lines for a period of rest and recreation at home. Uriah, of course, will sleep with Bathsheba, and when word is sent to the front lines a few weeks later that she is pregnant, Uriah will assume joyfully and without further thought that the child to be born is his own. End of problem for King David.

This is a clever scheme that has only one flaw: Uriah will not cooperate. A man of ultrasensitive conscience, he does not feel entitled to court the favors of Bathsheba while his army buddies in Charlie Company are still at the front courting death. So he does not spend the night in bed with his wife after all.

David, well acquainted with military life, and knowing what military men do on leave, has hardly expected loyalty to military comrades to outweigh the charms of Bathsheba. So he extends Uriah's leave for another day (and night). The fallback plan seems even more foolproof; he will ply Uriah with the king's best wines, and Uriah, after a sufficient number of rounds, his conscience numbed and his libido aroused, will race home from the banquet to have sex at least twice before returning to battle. But once again, Uriah, faithful to the plight of his less fortunate comrades-in-arms, spends the night not in his wife's arms but in the servants' quarters.

David is desperate. He knows that anybody who can count up to nine is going to figure out that the baby is not Uriah's. So in his desperation, David sends Uriah back to the front lines with a sealed envelope for his commander—a sealed envelope that contains his death warrant. Joab, the recipient of the sealed envelope, and Uriah's superior officer, is instructed by the king to see to it that Uriah dies in battle. Whatever Joab may think of the instructions, he knows, seasoned military man that he is, that "orders are orders" and that the head of state is also the commander-in-chief of the armed forces. He so arranges it that Uriah is killed by the Ammonites.

Word is relayed back to the palace. The commander-in-chief of the armed forces generously forgives Major Joab for the clumsy military maneuver that cost the life of his valiant Sergeant Uriah, and Sergeant Uriah is buried with full military honors and posthumously awarded the Legion of Valor. After the prescribed period of mourning for her dead husband, Bathsheba moves into the palace on the king's command, there is a betrothal ceremony and—a trifle prematurely, to be sure—a son is born to the happy royal couple. End of 2 Samuel 11.

Which is where "The David Story" might have ended, everything tidily back in place, had it not been for "The Nathan Story," which begins with 2 Samuel 12. We know a lot less about Nathan than about David, but we know enough to form some preliminary assessment of him before we meet him here (see 2 Sam. 7:1–17).

Nathan is one of the prophets in the king's court, which means that when the king has to make decisions, the retinue of prophets is supposed, by various means at its disposal, to inform the king of God's will. And any king with any sense will take his prophets seriously, for he would much prefer to have God on his side rather than on someone else's.

It didn't always work that way. Once, for example, David had wanted to build a temple to the Lord, and Nathan, responding to what he was told by the Lord, went out on a limb and indicated that David was not—repeat not—to build a temple. This took considerable courage on Nathan's part, not only because Nathan, in reporting God's will, was ranging himself against David's will—which is an uncomfortable position for a court prophet—but also because he had himself previously been part of the pro-temple crowd, urging David to go ahead with his construction plans, until the latest revelation from Yahweh had forced a change in the message he now had to communicate in his official prophetic status.

So Nathan, when we meet him in chapter 12, is not just some outsider who can stride on stage, deliver a blistering attack as the punch line to end act two, and leave forever. He has been on stage all the time, part of the royal household, a member of the inner circle. And those who break ranks within the inner circle are often tendered one-way tickets to the outer circle.

At the time we pick up the story, Nathan had survived that earlier crossing of the regal will, so he already has a bit of a track record of saying no to the king, although such an unpleasant task is not something a healthy man would want to face twice in a single lifetime.

No such luck for Nathan, however. He picks up the palace scuttlebutt as rapidly as the next person, which is that the hanky-panky between David and Bathsheba has not only involved adultery but also deception and murder. And by any standards of moral conduct, David is guilty on all three counts, only he doesn't know it. Somebody has to point this out, which is a clear entrance cue for a prophet. At this point, Nathan would probably have preferred to put in for a leave of absence, with or without pay, since calling a king to account, challenging the highest earthly authority one knows, is no small matter. Anyone who does so had better be committed to something or someone more ultimate than the king, be sure of all his facts, and possess a clear, well-modulated voice. Nathan apparently scored well in all three departments.

And Nathan, analogous to a military commander, is "under orders." That's what being a prophet is all about. The biblical text joining chapters 11 and 12 makes this clear: "But the thing that David had done displeased the LORD, and the LORD sent Nathan to David" (2 Sam. 11:27–12:1). Showdown time has come, and Nathan has to put all his security up for grabs.

"The Story of the Ewe Lamb" is the means by which Nathan traps the king into an admission of guilt. We need only notice how devastatingly David indicts himself out of his own mouth, and how Nathan responds.

Nathan's device is simplicity itself. He tells the king a story: Once upon a time there was a rich man with plenty of sheep. But when a guest came for dinner, the rich man stole the one ewe lamb that a poor man owned and loved, slaughtered it, and fed it to his guest. End of story.

David is indignant. Exclamation points fill the royal chamber. What injustice! What a travesty of human relations! Such a one should die! Let him at least repay the poor man fourfold for his gross theft of what belonged to another!

Nathan springs the trap. Four words are enough: "You are the man" (2 Sam. 12:7).

And that is really as far as we need to carry the tale, although Nathan goes on to make sure the point isn't lost, by pointing out certain analogies between the rich man, the poor man, the ewe lamb, and David, Uriah, and Bathsheba respectively. In any case, David sees the point and repents: "I have sinned against the LORD" (2 Sam. 12:13). A heavy price is paid: the fruit of the illicit relationship, a son, dies. But out of the union of David and Bathsheba comes another son, Solomon, who goes on to ambiguous heights of greatness as the successor in his father's dynasty.

And Nathan survives. It is not always the case that those who stand up against iniquity in high places survive, and those who plan to stand up against iniquity in high places had better not weave survival too centrally into their plans. That is why it is best to end the story with Nathan's ringing and unambiguous challenge to David, "You are the man, you are the one who has sinned, and you must be called to account, whatever the price" (2 Sam. 12:7, fleshed out).

The Story Part of Israel's Story

The overall story, while unique, does not stand alone. Its various components are often present in other parts of the canonical materials that contain it, though seldom with as much focused dramatic urgency. We can be reassured that we do not confront an isolated set of moral claims in this story, but only an exceptionally clear coming together of frequently voiced concerns.

As far as "the David Story" is concerned, there is a consistent enough witness against adultery throughout the Jewish scriptures so that the theme does not surprise us. As far as "the Ewe Lamb Story" is concerned, we have numerous instances in the Hebrew scripture of stories being used to make a point and even (in the case of the prophets) of metaphors that instead of being verbalized are enacted—the wearing of stocks or the smashing of cisterns—to transmit messages with special vividness. In the Christian scriptures, the telling of stories or parables is the most consistently used teaching device of Jesus of Nazareth. As far as "the Nathan Story" is concerned, it too represents a frequently repeated form of action in the Jewish scriptures. In fact, when we begin to work out from the present text, we discover that "the Nathan Syndrome" is all over the place. Standing up to authority wrongly exercised and saying a resounding no may be the most central story in the Hebrew scriptures, for it is actually a narrative rendering of the First Commandment, "You shall have no other gods before me" (Ex. 20:3). Since it is the particular temptation of kings and others in authority to conceive of themselves as slightly above the gods they are supposed to be serving, the challenge to idolatry becomes the major concern, if not quite the full-time job, of the Hebrew prophets.

But the concern is present long before the prophets. Indeed, it is at the heart of the paradigmatic biblical story, the story of the exodus, for here, too, kingly authority must be challenged. Moses stands up to the pharaoh, an act in some ways even braver than that of Nathan, for while Moses, like Nathan, was in control of his data, he did not have Nathan's clear, well-modulated voice. In fact, the Midrash reminds us, he stuttered badly and tried, unsuccessfully, to escape being Yahweh's mouthpiece, offering his speech impediment as a pretext for disengagement. But Moses was not allowed to cop out any more than was Nathan, which should be a consoling fact for those of us lacking oratorical skills; we can still be used.

The Power of a Story

What this story-within-a-story about David and Nathan reveals to us is the extraordinary extent to which *a story has power*. It is important to remember this whenever we are tempted to think of stories as no more than pleasant diversions from the sterner aspects of life, things we read to children or indulge in ourselves only when we've gotten caught up on the high priority items. I cannot attest to what goes on in Jewish or Catholic minds on this matter, but I can report that there are still Protestants who experience a lingering sense of unease when they turn to fiction instead of "serious reading."

Such an attitude sells the story form short. It is never as innocent as it appears—as King David had special reason to discover. Not only on Nathan's lips, but on many other lips and pages as well, stories have a surprising ability to sneak past our defenses and force us to look at things in a new way. One can imagine how tense David must have been when Nathan requested an audience, sure that Nathan had picked up the palace gossip and was about to denounce him. One can also imagine how relaxed David must have become when he heard Nathan begin with the lulling phrase, "Once upon a time. . . ." Entertainment, not judgment, was to be the order of the day.

As we have seen, however, the relief was short-lived; it did not turn out to be lulling time. For the story about an innocent ewe lamb was not really a story about an innocent ewe lamb, but about a guilty king, told in such a skillful way that David had been drawn too deeply into it to be able to extricate himself when he finally discovered what was going on.

It was Nathan's apparently artless (but consummately artful) comment, "You are the man," that broke down whatever remaining walls David might have wanted to retain between the two stories. By being brought into "the Ewe Lamb Story," David suddenly saw, in a sickening moment of insight, that he had been hearing not only "the Ewe Lamb Story" but "the David Story" as well, which up to that point had gone, "Kings-are-entitled-to-whatever-they-want-and-are-entitled-to-get-it-by-whatever-means-they-choose." In the light of "the Ewe Lamb Story," he encountered a revised version of his own story which now went, "Kings-are-as-accountable-as-anybody-else-when-they-do-wrong-and-they-must-pay-the- consequences-just-like-anybody-else."

The Power of the Story Now

There is another exercise the biblical passage commends to us, which further exemplifies the power of a story. It was remarked near the beginning of this chapter that persons like the ones who read this book are likely to hear 2 Samuel 11–12 as a strong indictment of adultery and see the passage as an occasion when individual moral failings are brought to the surface and perpetrators rendered accountable. That is not a theme to be discounted, but it is important to recall that many other readers, situated in circumstances quite different from those of most North Americans, read 2 Samuel 11–12 not only as a tale of judgment against individual iniquity but as a tale of empowerment for individual and social bravery, and as a model for the beginning of a new society.

These wide differences of interpretation are not occasioned by the story itself, since all listeners and readers share an identical text, but by the different situations and concerns that the various listeners and readers bring *to* the story. And one of the ways, in our shrinking world, that we can grasp the full flavor of such a tale is to read it, sympathetically and empathetically, from perspectives wider than our own, perspectives that force us to discover things within the story we would just as soon overlook.

The abuse of kingly power, for example, is not an item very high on the political or existential agendas of North Americans, and we do not initially hear the story speaking to us about such matters. But to those who are living in third-world dictatorships, the abuses of power to which David succumbed—claiming for himself whatever he wanted no matter to whom it belonged—are part and parcel of their everyday life. For forty years the Somoza family expropriated the peasants' lands in Nicaragua; for over ten years the Pinochet regime engaged in brutal denial of the human rights of Chilean citizens; for more years than Salvadorans care to remember, one military junta after another has been murdering citizens by the tens of thousands. From such situations, third-world readers who learn of David's exploits for personal gain and consolidation of power will know exactly what is going on.

To such people, the story will be not only a gloomy story about the abuses of power by others, but also, and more importantly, an exciting story about the assumption of power by themselves, because somebody stood up to the brutal abuse of power, named it, and even tamed it. The greatest problem for powerless people is their conviction that there is nothing they can do that will make a difference—which leads to apathy and despair. But the story of Nathan confronting David suggests an alternative to apathy and despair, and it is precisely the power of the story to make such a new vision possible. There can be new Nathans to confront the new Davids.

So far, so good: the story speaks with power to those in difficult situations. But does it say anything to North Americans who do not live in such straightened circumstances? The process we have been following indicates that it does, and that in at least two ways it can create a new moral intentionality for us as well.

First, as the story sensitizes us to the abuses of power by those in authority, we become more aware of ways in which David's abuse of power has analogies to abuses of power by our own authorities. Recent legislation extending through the lifetimes of public officials the need for administrative clearance before making any comments on political activity, total exclusion of the press from covering the invasion of Grenada along with military censorship in the U.S. invasions of Panama and Kuwait, the decision of the Reagan administration to administer random lie-detector tests to employees—these and other actions suggest that our own political leaders do not feel a need to be accountable to either national or international opinion. Such a mindset is similar to that of King David who, until challenged by Nathan, did not feel accountable to anyone beyond himself. As we reread the story, particularly in the light of its reading by third-world persons, we come to feel a new urgency about abuses of power at home.

The second concern comes unbidden to the surface of our minds in the light of ongoing exposure to the "David/Nathan/Ewe Lamb Story." As we ask ourselves (and even more as we are asked by third-world friends) about the resources that keep modern counterparts of David in power, we find ourselves forced to acknowledge that in each of the situations cited above (Somoza in Nicaragua, Pinochet in Chile, the succession of juntas in El Salvador), it has been the resources of our country—political, economic, military, clandestine—that have kept such regimes in power and legitimated their unjust activities.

At that point, the posture of Nathan assumes an even more pressing urgency. It is no longer enough to observe it from afar, or analyze it in an essay, or admire it in someone living far away. We have to entertain the uncomfortable possibility that we too must say to the Davids in our own land, "You are the man," and, even more, hear Nathan's words addressed to us, since to whatever degree we remain silent about, and therefore complicit in, the actions of a government that acts in our name, we too become those who can only be described in the imagery of rich men with many flocks, who are systematically taking from poor men and women the paltry store of goods they have.

It may seem as though this chapter, which started as a piece of literary analysis, is ending as political commentary. I submit, however, that the direction the chapter has taken verifies its main point, namely that stories have power to challenge us and engage us, and that they may lead us in directions we never intended to go. On one level of my being I would prefer to stay on the less threatening terrain of literary analysis, but the nature of the story makes an excursion into contemporary politics necessary. Just as Nathan challenged the structure of power gone askew in his own day, so must we challenge the structure of power gone askew in our own day.

The power of a story is a power over which we do not have ultimate control, since it can catch us off guard, tell us things about ourselves we would prefer not to know, and liberate us to move in directions we would never have imagined.

2

CUT FLOWERS, SELECTIVE GRATITUDE, AND ASSYRIANS IN MODERN DRESS

We should be constantly amazed that authors can put curious, arbitrarily chosen markings on a page (what we call "letters"), and that appropriate combinations of these letters can cause people to weep, rejoice, throw in the towel, become intensely political, or enter a monastery. It is surely cause for wonder that we can read words about another person or era, even an imaginary person or era "existing" only in the mind of someone else, situated a hundred years in the past or a thousand years in the future, and come to the inescapable conclusion, *"This concerns me."* Refinement of the conclusion can go in many directions: "If this is so, I've been wrong about a lot of things." Or, "I've been right about a few things." Or, "I've got to change." Or, just to round things out, "How delightful!"—for along with everything else, we are entitled to moments of sheer rejoicing, quite apart from their "relevance."

The more we reflect on it, the more complicated and mysterious it all becomes. And the complications and mysteries are magnified tenfold when reflection takes the form of "This has something to do (for good or ill) with my religious faith." Here again the options are numerous. What I read may challenge my faith drastically. It may confirm it healingly. It may complicate it surprisingly. It may annihilate it permanently. More than likely it will do some or all of the above in different proportions on different occasions. At all events, whoever attempts to look at life from a faith perspective finds that the world of fiction and the world of faith cannot be hermetically sealed off from each other.

For example, the recent catalogue of a religious publishing house contains several pages of book titles under the heading "Christian Fiction," followed by a shorter section of book titles under the heading "Interesting Fiction." Many people seem content to keep the divorce permanent.

On one side are those who look with suspicion on books described as "Christian fiction," fearing (as we saw in chapter 1) that any piece of literature thus labeled will be no more than thinly disguised propaganda, with characters so manipulated and plot so contrived that an "improving" moral conclusion can be guaranteed.

In brief rebuttal, it may be suggested that there is a crucial difference between a self-styled "Christian novelist" (who may, indeed, be a propagandist), and an author who also happens to be a Christian, just as another author might be a humanist or a Marxist or an agnostic. Such writers (as we will see in our discussions of Alan Paton and Frederick Buechner) put the integrity of their craft above contriving plots that will score points for particular religious positions.

On the other side, however, are Christians who, while not unhappy when fiction is "interesting," remain fearful that too many forays outside the Christian tent will leave them in a spiritual desert or wasteland. Consequently, they would rather keep their sights narrow and their faith secure than breathe pagan air and run the risk of spiritual asphyxiation. These persons frequently profess to be upset by the seamy side of life communicated in so many contemporary novels. Such earnest folk need to be reminded that their own Holy Scriptures are replete with stories of adultery, infidelity, murder, suicide, intrigue, disloyalty, and any other human shortcomings one cares to itemize. Modern novelists have no monopoly on descriptions of sin.

If, in distinction from the above attempts, we seek to deal with the potentially creative interplay between fiction and faith, there are at least three ways to formulate such a response, and I will describe them in what I perceive to be an ascending order of importance. The issue, to put it a little too grandly, goes, How is it possible to see the hand of God in the work of non-Christian writers? Or, a little less grandly, How can the life of faith be nurtured by literature that is not specifically a product of that faith?

First Claim: Christianity Has Influenced Culture

An initial response to these questions is to assert that non-Christian writers, whether they acknowledge it or not, have been nurtured in a cultural milieu formed by Christian convictions, and have—even unconsciously—absorbed many of the values for which that culture stands, values they communicate through their writings, whether in Christian terms or not.

The argument does not always work when the writers are Chinese or Korean or African, unless one wants to insist that Western colonialism transmitted "Christian values" to other cultures—an insistence that would be difficult to prove, and, in terms of the actual fruits of colonialism, hardly a creative tribute to Christian faith and human understanding.

Nor does the argument work much better on our own cultural scene, unless we state it in the past tense. That Christianity *did* influence the culture of Europe and then North America is a claim to which it would be difficult to take exception, and examples abound. But that it still does so is open to serious debate, for much of society has become emancipated from most of its earlier Christian roots. An image that helps to describe this situation is that of a flower severed from its roots and placed in a vase. The flower will survive for a limited time, during which its bloom can be appreciated, but every observer knows it will finally die.

If most contemporary writers do not affirm the Christian roots imbedded in culture, they nevertheless admire and even cherish many of the blooms those roots created, and they can describe them in depth, sometimes very lovingly. Most of them would probably describe Western culture as "post-Christian" and work within it to appraise its strengths and weaknesses without dependence upon, or reference to, Christianity.

Examples of such secondary inheritance are the treatments of human nature that we find in contemporary fiction. It is part of the classical Christian legacy to our world, first, that all human beings are created in the image of God and are thus of infinite worth; second, that "all have sinned and come short of the glory of God," a fact that comes as close to being empirically verifiable as any part of the Christian dispensation; and third, that there is always the possibility for human beings to "turn about" and start living in new ways, empowered to do so by God working within them. Most contemporary authors eschew the traditional vocabulary that has gone along with such an estimate of human nature (original sin, the Fall, conversion, regeneration, "reliance on the grace of God," and so forth), but it is undeniable that most writers of fiction today are describing people, often in graphic detail, who are at any one of the above three stages of the traditional Christian story. Many of the fruits of faith survive even if the roots are gone:

The effect of the three facets of the Christian legacy on writers is shown by the following, corresponding, examples. Some authors fall in love with their characters and see them as having infinite worth (John Updike once accused J. D. Salinger of loving his characters more than God loved them), and they lavish great care on them—without even passing attention to the notion that their worth is somehow attributable to the image of God within each of them. Many more authors describe vividly the chicaneries of their characters, the ugly things they do, the deceptions to which once "good" people stoop to save their own skins, and so on—without any sense that their characters are, by their misdeeds, defying God or at least the moral order, as well as their fellow human beings. And a few authors, the very best, wrestle with how the results of human misdeeds can somehow be turned to good account—without any reference to the enabling power of the grace of God, or regeneration, or atonement or conversion.

The above paragraph is offered not judgmentally or accusingly but descriptively, and seeks only to propose that any kind of direct influence of "Christian culture" on modern writers is likely to be tenuous.

If it is true that the Christian roots out of which concern for humanity was once based have almost disappeared, if the original divine light has been extinguished (or at least is perceived no more) and we are now living only in the afterglow, it is anybody's guess what the future holds. If the bloom is indeed leaving the flower, we have at least three options: (a) we can hasten the process by cynically deeming the flower expendable; (b) we can lavish care upon it to prolong its life and loveliness as long as possible, extolling its beauty the more gratefully since we know its days are numbered; or (c) we can try despairingly yet admirably to build a culture that is *not* dependent on earlier roots, seeking stimuli that will make possible the flower's rebirth out of resources we are still seeking to create.

In any case, the distance that now lies between the Christian impulses and contemporary writers is too great for Christians to make confident assertions that their faith is still the implicit if not explicit dynamic behind modern fiction.

Second Claim: Truth Is to Be Welcomed Whatever Its Source

Another way of relating the insights of contemporary writers to the Christian faith can be found as early as the second century. Early Christian apologists, as they were called, had to come to terms with the fact that the pagans had said a lot of very true things without appealing to Christian revelation, and as a result many apologists maintained a fairly genial relationship with classical culture. Justin Martyr, for example, could claim, "Whatever has been well said anywhere or by anyone belongs to us Christians" (*Apology,* II, 13). This was not so much an act of triumphalism as of gratitude: since all truth was one, and all truth came from God, any manifestation of the truth was a manifestation of God at work, whatever the philosophical or ideological garb in which it was clothed. Augustine elaborates the point:

> All branches of heathen learning have not only false and superstitious fancies . . . but they contain also liberal instruction which is better adapted to the use of truth, and some most excellent precepts of morality; and some truths in regard even to the worship of the one God are found among them. Now these are, so to speak, their gold and silver, which they did not create themselves, but dug out of the mines of God's providence which are everywhere scattered abroad. (*De Doctrina Christiana*, II, xl)

Lest it be suspected that Protestant orthodoxy remained aloof from such bridge building, there is corroboration for a generous acknowledgment of the achievements of pagan writers in John Calvin:

> Whenever, therefore, we meet with heathen writers, let us learn from that light of truth which is admirably displayed in their works, that the human mind, fallen as it is, and corrupted from its integrity, is yet invested and adorned by God with excellent talents. If we believe that the Spirit of God is the only fountain of truth, we shall neither reject nor despise the truth itself, *wherever it shall appear,* unless we wish to insult the Spirit of God. (*Institutes,* II, ii, xv, italics added)

In more recent times, the late Archbishop of Canterbury, William Temple, came to much the same conclusion after an examination of the prologue to the fourth Gospel. The prologue deals with the Word of God, the *Logos,* the creative power of God, the Word that has become flesh and dwelt among us, so that God's creative activity is now manifest on the human scene. That Christ was for him the agent of all creativity, made it possible for Archbishop Temple to put a high value, therefore, on every expression of creativity:

> By the Word of God—that is to say, by Jesus Christ—Isaiah, and Plato, and Zoroaster, and Buddha, and Confucius conceived and uttered such truths as they declared. There is only one divine light, and every man is in his measure enlightened by it. (William Temple, *Readings in St. John's Gospel,* p. 10)

The implication of such a position in relation to creative literature can be indicated by revising the sentences quoted above so that they read, "By the Word of God . . . Updike, and Steinbeck, and Faulkner, and Kafka, and Carson McCullers conceived and uttered such truths as they declared. There is only one light, and all authors in their measure are enlightened by it" (William Temple, revised).

The conclusion to be drawn is not that the existence of Updike, Steinbeck, and company proves that Christianity is really on the ball after all, but rather that Christians must listen to them more sympathetically than they usually do.

God's concerns are not limited solely to "Christian thinkers," or people within the church, and there must be proper humility on the part of Christians in the face of the fact that non-Christians can be vehicles of God's truth also.

But the position has a flaw, which, if not fatal, is serious. It is that under this arrangement, Christian appropriation of non-Christian literature and insights is likely to be no more than a piecemeal affair. Rather than hearing the authors on their own terms, Christians are tempted to lift from given authors only those things that are congenial to a Christian view, and to ignore the rest, thus mutilating the author's full message. The same process is graphically at work when a publisher excerpts from a negative book review three or four words which, when taken out of context and surrounded by ellipses, appear to praise the book, and uses them in subsequent advertising. All authors have a right to be outraged at such treatment, whether by overzealous publishers or overzealous Christians, since their own convictions are either being inaccurately communicated or shunted aside.

Third Claim: Contemporary Writers Are Assyrians in Modern Dress

Is there a way to avoid the difficulties in the above two positions of claiming too much and claiming too selectively? If so, it would have to be based on a conviction that God can use *all* things for the fulfillment of the divine purposes, including the *full* message of non-Christians rather than only selected congenial portions. Christians will have to be willing to hear not only words that are apparently congruent with Christian faith but also words that clearly are not.

It is this approach that the image of "Assyrians in modern dress" seeks to affirm. The role of the Assyrian is laid out in a remarkable passage in the book of Isaiah (ch. 10:5–11). The Israelites (self-styled as "God's people") are being besieged by the pagan Assyrians, who from Isaiah's initial perspective are distinctly *not* "God's people." The conventional pattern in such situations is threefold: the prophet is to (a) call down God's judgment on the pagans, (b) gird Israel to be the agent through whom God's power and might can be displayed to the pagans, in order (c) to bring about a suitable repentance all around, and possibly even some transfers of real estate as a sign of good faith.

But in Isaiah 10, the author unexpectedly reverses this scenario. Since God has become more than a little impatient with Israel's cumulative infidelities, it is Israel, rather than Assyria, on whom the divine wrath will be focused. Not only that, but Assyria itself will be God's instrument for announcing and carrying out this unexpected turn of events. God reflects:

Ah, Assyria, the rod of my anger—
  the club in their hands is my fury!
Against a godless nation I send him . . .
                    (Isa. 10:5–6)

The "godless nation" is not Assyria but Israel. It is a scandalous notion. Israel has failed the test, but this failure, rather than thwarting God's purposes, opens the way for God to use other means to demonstrate who is running the store and call Israel back into allegiance to God.

We must not fail to note that what makes Assyria so powerful a witness against Israel is precisely its unbelief. Isaiah never says that Assyria is to be taken seriously only at those points where Israel and Assyria agree. Assyria must be listened to and reckoned with as Assyria, as nonbeliever. *Assyria must be seen and heard on Assyria's terms, not Israel's.*

This is the stance from which Christians can most profitably look upon contemporary novelists today—as Assyrians in modern dress, who must first of all be allowed to speak *as themselves,* with their own full voices, heard on their own terms. Christians need not claim that non-Christian writers are some kind of closet Christians, nor need Christians appropriate from their writings only what is congruent with a Christian stance. (By so asserting, we defuse the two strategies sketched earlier.) That they might somehow be vehicles of God's revelation to Christians may sound surprising (to the Assyrians as well as to the Christians), but it is no more surprising than the original notion that pagan Assyria was a vehicle of God's revelation to the Israelites.

That is novel enough, but the Isaiah passage suggests something even more novel. From the perspective of any modern Isaiah in the crowd, the word the Assyrians speak will not only be a word from them, it will also be a word from God. Such a claim may sound unreasonable to Christians and preposterous to Assyrians, so we must note how Isaiah deals with it. After asserting that God makes use of pagan Assyria to announce the divine will to Israel, Isaiah goes on realistically to concede that it never enters Assyria's mind that it is being so used by God (a God in whom Assyria does not even believe), and that the Assyrian king would have been either amused at, or contemptuous of, such a suggestion: "He does not so intend, and his mind does not so think" (Isa. 10:7, RSV).

Modern writers, from this perspective, can be used by God even though they do not so intend and their minds do not so think (Isa. 10:7, revised). They, too, like Nebuchadnezzar, may be amused at, or contemptuous of, such descriptions of themselves. But this heightens their importance rather than lessening it. For they have at least three things to say to Christians that Christians cannot seem to hear from one another:

1. Modern Assyrians make an important contribution to Christians by portraying, in all of its starkness, *a world without grace,* a world in which the promises of faith have not been heard and may not even have been announced. Modern writers are particularly well suited to portray such a world, since for many of them it is their habitation. Here, for example, is Tennessee Williams, in the preface to his play *The Rose Tattoo,* starting out to talk about pity and love, and finding that only three sentences later he must talk about fear and evasion:

> Men pity and love each other more deeply than they permit themselves to know. The moment after the phone has been hung up, the hand reaches for a scratch pad and scrawls a notation: "Funeral Tuesday at five, Church of the Holy Redeemer, don't forget flowers." And the same hand is only a little shakier than usual as it reaches, some minutes later, for a highball glass that will pour a stupefaction over the kindled nerves. Fear and evasion are the two little beasts that chase each other's tail in the revolving wire-cage of our nervous world. They distract us from feeling too much about things. Time rushes toward us with its hospital tray of infinitely varied narcotics, even while it is preparing us for its inevitably fatal operation.

There is an honesty here that does not take refuge in pious evasions or platitudes but is willing to look at life without blinders or other protective devices. Anything Christianity has to say about the human condition and ways to transform it must take the perception of Tennessee Williams into account.

2. But for Christians, the immersion must be even deeper. Modern Assyrians challenge Christians (and all religiously minded people) *to recast their complacent forms of faith,* by insisting that, as a prerequisite for the right to proclaim, they must themselves go through the depths of disbelief with those for whom faith has not spoken a healing word. They must be our guides in a contemporary descent into hell, which, in the hell the modern world has become, must be gone through if there is ever to be a resurrection. We are called upon to entertain their vision, to run the risk of standing with them, so that we may see everything they see (the bad along with the good) and receive no prior assurances that there is more to see than they describe for us.

We can be sure that faith will not emerge unscathed from such a venture. But a faith fearful of attack is hardly a faith worth having, and better that it be demolished than that it fortify a world of illusion. Commenting on the artistic achievement of T. S. Eliot, Amos Wilder writes:

> Dante traverses all the circles of Hell to know what Paradise means, and this Hell was not a private one alone, but the inferno of a whole age and of many cities and courts. T. S. Eliot's great achievement rests on the fact that he has himself been initiated into the furies and stagnations of our age and of its cities. (*Otherworldliness and the New Testament,* p. 31)

An initiation into the "furies and stagnations of our age and of its cities" is one of the gifts promised us by the modern Assyrians. Some, indeed, offer us much more, but if they do, it is only because they too have accepted that bitter initiation. There is no doubt that faith undergoes challenge and even attack at the hand of the modern Assyrians, but a faith that enters the fray with openness and courage has the possibility of emerging a stronger faith, dignifying rather than debasing the name. Assyrians who force us to this extremity can be God's instruments, and are God's instruments, whether they will it or no. They must not be expected to carry us over the great gulf that separates belief from unbelief. But they can take us to the brink of that gulf and show it to us. They may not be bearers of grace, but they may at least be preparers for it.

3. Christians also need help from the Assyrians in modern dress in *how best to address their message* to others. This means not only dialectical skills but artistic skills as well (theologians are not noted for being captivating stylists). Human predicaments which Christians and Assyrians existentially share are often stated more clearly and persuasively by the latter than by the former. Arthur Miller's play *The Death of a Salesman,* first performed in 1949, has recently been revived, and its themes are as "modern" as they were over forty years ago. Miller wrote of the issues that face Willy Loman, and face all of us: "[The problem of the play is] the fear that one has lied to oneself over a period of years in relation to one's true identity and what one should be doing in the world." The play makes people ask themselves whether their rationalizations about themselves are not leading them to "an ultimate rendezvous with a dreadful reckoning." These are cosmic themes, which means that they are theological and eschatological themes: "one's true destiny . . . what one should be doing in the world . . . an ultimate rendezvous with a dreadful reckoning." It would be hard to improve on Arthur Miller's understanding of the core questions that are at the center of each human life, and Christians as well as non-Christians should resonate to them.

John Steinbeck's *East of Eden* provides another statement of the idea that we can be caught in the struggle between good and evil, and have to take account of that in the living of our lives:

> I believe that there is one story in the world, and only one. . . . Human beings are caught—in their lives, in their thoughts, in their hungers and ambitions, in their avarice and cruelty, and in their kindness and generosity too—in a net of good and evil. I think this is the only story we have and that it occurs on all levels of feeling and intelligence. Virtue and vice were warp and woof of our first consciousness, and they will be the fabric of our last, and this despite any changes we may impose on field and river and mountain, on economy and manners. . . .

> We have only one story. All novels, all poetry, are built on the never-ending contest in ourselves of good and evil. And it occurs to me that evil must constantly respawn, while good, while virtue, is immortal. Vice has always a new fresh young face, while virtue is venerable as nothing else in the world is.

Not all are as hopeful as Steinbeck. The struggle between good and evil may be so desperate that redemption is hard to come by and can be no more than hinted at. Robert Penn Warren measured human evil to its depths as a gateway toward new human possibilities. His long verse poem *Brother to Dragons* has lost none of its biting power over the years. In it, the author recounts a discussion, in some kind of limbo, between himself, Thomas Jefferson, and other members of the Jefferson family. The discussion concerns the brutal murder of a slave by one of Jefferson's relatives, Lilburn Lewis, who hacked the slave to pieces with a meat axe because he had broken a pitcher belonging to Lilburn's mother. Warren, struck by the fact that none of Jefferson's writings mention this incident, confronts him with the event. Jefferson is unable to square the murder with his deistic, optimistic doctrine of human nature. The cold fact, and Jefferson's nice theory, simply will not jibe. And Jefferson is forced to recast his view of human nature in the light of what took place on Lilburn's plantation. He has to take seriously the fact of human sin as it exists in Lilburn.

And not only as it exists in Lilburn. . . . Warren sees more deeply than that. As he talks with all the characters in any way related to the event, it becomes clear that they all share in the guilt of what has happened. And then Warren reminds his readers that they too were in the hut, participating in that brutal murder: "We have lifted the meataxe in the elation of love and justice." He goes on:

> We have lain on the bed and devised evil in the heart.
> We have stood in the sunlight and named the bad thing good and the good
>   thing bad.

But Warren does not simply end on this negative note. There is another side to the story, which Warren both honors and explicates in five trenchant lines that argue what he calls "the necessity of virtue":

> The recognition of complicity is the beginning of innocence.
> The recognition of necessity is the beginning of freedom.
> The recognition of the direction of fulfillment
>   is the death of the self.
> And the death of the self is the beginning of selfhood.
> All else is surrogate of hope and destitution of spirit.
>   (*Brother to Dragons*, pp. 214–215)

So if this is a poem about "original sin," it is rather close to what G. K. Chesterton, in a typical paradox, called "the good news of original sin," a recognition that while we are sinners, we are not only sinners but those for whom the possibility of redemption is always present. When we read Warren's words "the death of the self is the beginning of selfhood," it should not be surprising if we hear somewhere an echo of the words, "You must be born again."

3

FOUR WAYS OF WAITING
A Case Study
(J. D. Salinger, Samuel Beckett,
Franz Kafka, W. H. Auden)

"**O**urs is a time of waiting," Paul Tillich wrote in *The Shaking of the Foundations*, "waiting is its special destiny." The words are as true today as they were when he wrote them over forty years ago.

The observation may be a breath of hope or an utterance of despair, depending on the nature of that for which (or for whom) we believe our time is waiting. It is clear enough that our age does not exude confidence or claim to possess much truth. To whatever degree past ages had assurances about the nature of tomorrow or the nature of the ultimate, those assurances are no longer available to most people today, and no new assurances have arisen to take their place save for faiths that have been exposed as pseudo-faiths—faith in a millennium to arrive once the class struggle has been resolved, or faith in a millennium to arrive as soon as we can get government to stop meddling with a free-enterprise economy.

This is not a unique situation in human history. Commenting on their plight as they were forced out of the Garden of Eden, Adam is depicted in a *New Yorker* cartoon as comforting Eve with the words, "My dear, we live in an age of transition." Adam and Eve, "man" and "woman," wait in every age, poised between a lost paradise and a dark unknown. Sometimes they say in hope with Simeon, "Mine eyes have seen thy salvation" (Luke 2:30, RSV), but more often they say in despair with Hezekiah, "This is a day of distress, of rebuke, and of disgrace; children have come to birth, and there is no strength to bring them forth" (2 Kings 19:3, RSV).

But the theme of waiting need not be pursued solely in biblical terms. It has attracted the attention of modern writers as well, and treatments of the theme of waiting reveal the extent to which they are dealing with themes that are theological in content and concern, whether they would grace them with such an adjective or not.

Waiting Casually

A common type of waiting is the attitude of waiting casually, adopting a stance designed to imply that nothing monumental is at stake. The fact that it is usually contrived suggests that it does not reveal true inner feelings but is a way of hiding true inner feelings. J. D. Salinger has given a classic description of such masked anticipation in the person of Lane Coutell, the terrifyingly conventional undergraduate in *Franny and Zooey*. As the 10:52 arrives at the New Haven station, bringing on it the girls who are coming for a Yale weekend,

> the door to the waiting room banged open, and the boys who had been keeping themselves warm began to come out to meet the train, most of them giving the impression of having at least three lighted cigarettes in each hand.
> Lane himself lit a cigarette as the train pulled in. Then, like so many people, who, perhaps, ought to be issued only a very probational pass to meet trains, he tried to empty his face of all expression that might quite simply, perhaps even beautifully, reveal how he felt about the arriving person.

Not many people can really pull this off, and even Lane Coutell's blasé composure and studied disinterest are vulnerable, in part at least, because Franny is *not* wearing a mask:

> "Lane!" Franny greeted him pleasurably—and she was not one for emptying her face of expression. She threw her arms around him and kissed him. It was a station-platform kiss—spontaneous enough to begin with, but rather inhibited in the follow-through, and with something of a forehead-bumping aspect.

Waiting in Doubt

When things are more consequential than an Ivy League weekend, however, casual waiting is not a true possibility. Much more widespread, if still confused, is an attitude that might be described, clumsily but accurately, as waiting-for-we-know-not-what-but-realizing-that-whatever-it-is,-it-might-be-pretty-damned-important.

It may be that this is the kind of waiting most characteristic of our age. We cannot resurrect past answers, and we cannot rest content with the confusions of the present, but we still haven't a clue as to what the future will bring, even though we know it must bring something and that whatever it brings might affect us deeply.

This attitude of waiting in doubt (to abbreviate the term to more manageable length) is mirrored almost perfectly in Samuel Beckett's play *Waiting for Godot*. Two tramps wait for "Godot" to appear. He never does. That two-sentence summary encompasses plot, action, subplot, and theme.

The very ambiguity in the play's title is revealing. Who is "Godot"? Nobody is sure, least of all the critics, and Beckett refuses to let easy or conclusive answers to the question emerge. The initial thought that Godot is God is temporarily reinforced by a reference, with Matthean overtones, to his caring for sheep and goats, but the purveyor of that information later tells us that Godot "does nothing." When Pozzo comes on stage it is conjectured both times that perhaps he is "Godot." When we remember that the play, first written in French, was titled *En Attendant Godot,* we are forced to recall that words associated in that language with "Godot" are such words as *godenot, godichon, godelureau,* and the like, words that have the connotation not of divinity but of awkwardness: runt, lout, country bumpkin, and the like.

The identification of Godot with God in so many analyses of the play is surely predicated on Beckett's extensive use of Christian imagery. There are constant references to Christ, to the cross, to salvation and damnation, but the interesting (and disquieting) thing is that these images become radically ambiguous. Beckett says more to us about the cross than most modern sermons do, and yet it is a cross without power to save. A long speech by Lucky has embedded within it fragments of the Christian message of salvation: ". . . a personal God . . . who from the heights of divine *apatheia* . . . loves us dearly . . . and suffers." But the brilliantly parodic speech indicates that this message can no longer be affirmed as a significant word.

The highly ambiguous nature of any Christian input is further highlighted by a statement of Saint Augustine that, according to Amos Wilder, gave Beckett the idea for the play: "One of the thieves crucified beside Christ went to heaven; do not despair. The other went to hell; do not presume." This theme particularly intrigues Didi in the early moments of the play, but since all four evangelists speak of the fate of the thieves and only one of the four suggests that a thief was saved, the odds are hardly encouraging and the matter is dropped.

It is clear that Gogo and Didi do not know for whom they are waiting. Expectation and hope have almost entirely vanished: "Nothing happens, nobody comes, nobody goes, it's awful." *And yet they wait.* Indeed, at the end of each act they propose to give up waiting and move on: "Well, shall we go?" "Yes, let's go." But the concluding line of each act is the stage direction, "They do not move," and that repeated stage direction is the most hopeful note in the play. They may wait without assurance ("He didn't say for sure he'd come"), but at least they wait.

The thing that makes all the waiting bearable is perhaps the fact that they wait together. If God seems infinitely remote, then the most they can do is draw near to one another. Even waiting-for-we-know-not-what might be tolerable if it is not waiting in total isolation.

The above comments describe not only Gogo and Didi but ourselves as well. Many moderns recoil from the notion that they are mirrored in Beckett's filthy tramps, but it is only the external trappings that make the identification suspect. We may not be infected with lice as they are, our landscape may include more than a barren tree, and we may not be hungry, but beyond such incidentals we are rather accurately portrayed. For we, too, are waiting, and we, too, do not know the formless and faceless "Godot" for whom we are waiting. We, too, must relieve the boredom of waiting: where Gogo and Didi have carrots and turnips, we indulge in *hors d'oeuvres* and cocktails; where they look for lice, we exterminate termites from split-level ranch houses; where they talk and fight, we too talk and fight, even if about different things. But it all has the same purpose, whether it is we or they: to relieve the boredom, so that we can be, as T. S. Eliot wrote in "Burnt Norton," "distracted from distraction by distraction." And surely we too find our refuge and solace in the fact that we wait together. Having lost a vision of the city of God, we strive to shore up the foundations of an independent city of humanity, and we do this a little more frantically each decade since we can no longer quite beg the primal question of whether or not the city of humanity, apart from the city of God, has any true substance.

Waiting in Dread

Were we truly to face that primal question, the nature of our waiting might be drastically altered. Rather than waiting casually, or waiting for we know not what, we would be waiting in dread.

This brand of waiting has been described—and lived—by Franz Kafka. Kafka spent his whole life waiting. He was a Jew but not a practicing Jew, "the servant of a God not believed in," as Franz Blei described him. He did not believe in the God of Judaism, but he did believe in "the Indestructible," something bearing in upon him, impinging upon him, before which he felt guilt. He was Job without God, living with a sense of what Nathan Scott has called "cosmic exile," a realm that all his characters likewise inhabit.

Kafka's sense of the utter incongruity between humanity and the Indestructible is reminiscent of Karl Barth, a Protestant theologian, who described God as the Totally Other, and who, following Kierkegaard (who also influenced Kafka), spoke of "the infinitely qualitative distinction between God and man." For Barth, however, the Totally Other had come near in Jesus Christ, fully indwelling a human life, so that the contemplation of God became progressively a joy rather than a terror. But for Kafka, that gap, that yawning abyss which could not be bridged from the human side, was not bridged from the other side either. And so Kafka's characters, and Kafka himself, inhabit an alien universe to which they are accountable. The result is an overpowering sense of guilt. And this in turn means that human beings wait in dread, for judgment must be pronounced on guilt. This is the situation reflected in Kafka's two most important novels, *The Trial* and *The Castle*.

Each describes the situation of a man who is waiting. In the first, Joseph K is summoned to trial by the court, but he waits throughout the entire book to find out precisely what the charges against him are. He never does. It is an ongoing nightmare. Moreover, the court with which Joseph K has to deal is without the well-ordered procedures we have come to associate with the law. His court is dirty, ill-kept, stupidly bureaucratic, and unwilling to clarify the charges under discussion. No matter how hard Joseph K tries to find out the nature of his crime, he remains at the mercy of the court, waiting for a clarification that never comes. Since he cannot discover the charges, he cannot prepare a defense. Finally he is summoned by two assassins who put him to death, and he dies with the words "Like a dog!" issuing from his throat.

In *The Castle*, K, a land-surveyor, comes to a town on the way to a castle where he has been appointed to a responsible position. But he never gets there. When he tries to find the way he is led astray. When he waits for instructions to arrive, they do not come. When he finally gets a phone call through, the conversation is so garbled as to be no help at all. All he can do is wait—anticipating instructions, anticipating a message, anticipating a resolution of the strange situation in which his relationship to the castle becomes increasingly confused. But the instructions, the message, the resolution, are never forthcoming. All he can do is wait.

The book, significantly, was never finished, nor was its predecessor. This may tell us that Kafka did not want sheer waiting to be the last word, but it also tells us that he had no alternative to offer in its place. He exposes false answers, yet with agonizing honesty is unable to offer further options. He shows, for example, the utter inadequacy of the well-ordered life, for it is the well-ordered life that is judged and found wanting. At the beginning of *The Trial*, Joseph K is a good example of an Organization Man. He is hard-working, ambitious, devoid of "outside interests" that might interfere with his advancement. And all that is precisely what is called into question. Joseph K does not know by whom it is called into question, and he does not know what to do about it, but it is clear that everything his life has represented is being called to judgment.

To be sure, he attempts to cope with the charges. He begins by denying their reality. He asserts his innocence. The most he will concede is that there has been a "misunderstanding," even when a priest responds with the disquieting comment, "All guilty people talk like that." Later, he tries to exploit "connections" on his behalf—Huld the advocate, and Titorelli, the "insider" with special information. But so great is the cumulative oppressiveness that there comes for Joseph K a curious and reluctant recognition that the court *has* some kind of claim over him. He has enough of an "uneasy conscience" to realize that there is something more ultimate than the well-ordered life, if only he could discover what it is. In an aphorism that Joseph Tauber describes as paraphrasing the whole of the novel, Kafka describes the two sides of the human situation:

> A certain heaviness, a feeling of being secured against every vicissitude, the vague assurance of a bed prepared for him and belonging to him alone, kept him from getting up; but he is kept from lying still by an unrest which drives him from his bed, by his conscience, the endless beating of his heart, the fear of death and the longing to refute it; all this will not let him rest and he gets up again.

There is, then, in all the waiting in dread, a dim fear that the court has legitimate claims against the individual, however hard it may be to determine precisely what they are. There is an overhanging sense of judgment: "Only our concept of time," Kafka writes, "makes it possible for us to speak of the Day of Judgment by that name; in reality it is a summary court in perpetual session."

This is a long way from the well-ordered life. Those who think themselves satisfied with the well-ordered life are living only on the surface, a surface so thin that it is liable to be punctured at any moment, as it was in Joseph K's case. And the verdict is: guilty. The more Joseph K tries to establish his innocence the more he becomes aware of his inexpungible guilt. He dies "like a dog," apparently almost happy at the "justice" of an ignominious death at the hand of the two assassins.

Is there an alternative to this? There is certainly none in *The Trial*. But there is a hint in *The Castle*, or at least in the circumstances surrounding its writing. The two novels, indeed, pose the alternatives in their purest form: either guilt or grace. There are no other options.

In a penetrating essay on Kafka in *The Myth of Sisyphus*, Albert Camus remarks, "*The Trial* propounds a problem which *The Castle*, to a certain degree, solves. The first describes according to a quasi-scientific method and without concluding. The second, to a certain degree, explains. *The Trial* diagnoses, and *The Castle* imagines a treatment." Kierkegaard wrote in *Purity of Heart,* "earthly hope must be killed; only then can one be saved by true hope," which Camus says can be translated, "One has to have written *The Trial* to undertake *The Castle.*" It is clear that in the latter, as in the former, there is no hope on the human side. There is only increasing frustration, for K does not get to the castle. As was indicated earlier, Kafka never finished the novel and never resolved the problem. But Kafka's close friend and editor, Max Brod, hints at a "solution":

> Kafka never wrote the concluding chapter. But he told me about it once when I asked him how the novel was to end. The ostensible Land Surveyor was to find partial satisfaction at least. He was not to relax in his struggle, but was to die worn out by it. Round his death bed the villagers were to assemble, and from the Castle itself the word was to come that though K's legal claim to live in the Castle was not valid, yet, taking certain auxiliary circumstances into account, he was to be permitted to live and work there.

Now to say this is certainly to shift the accent in the description of waiting. For Kafka, the waiting is indeed a waiting in dread, through the whole of *The Trial* and through all of *The Castle* that was committed to paper. But in the latter we see that for one who faces "the Indestructible" and who measures to all its depth the charge of "guilty," there is at least a shadow of grace, a hint of hope. It will not be of our doing, and it will not be recognizable, until all the resources that comprise our doing have been explored and rejected.

Interlude: Is It Possible to Move Beyond Dread?

Can the waiting in dread, then, be transformed into a waiting in hope? For Kafka, the transition was not possible save in fragmentary form. The terms in which it might have been possible are focused in the Judaism he could not accept and in the Christianity that has sprung from it.

Judaism does not diminish, but rather accentuates the poignancy of Kafka's description of human lostness. From one point of view, Judaism is a kind of parable of our human situation. That is to say, Jews in particular often feel alienated from other human beings and live in a state of exile from them, just as human beings in general often feel alienated from the cosmos and live in a state of exile from it. In terms of this imagery, Kafka is a Jew lost in the desert looking for a Promised Land he cannot believe in, and in this plight he epitomizes the plight of humanity.

But here is the point at which Kafka's vision is transcended by the religion
of his forebears. For the Jews are no longer lost in the desert; they were led to
the Promised Land. To be sure, they were later exiled from it, but they learned
to see a meaning even in their exile, and to discern the hand of God, not absent
but present, in the midst of their deepest distress. And so Judaism came to
represent a waiting in hope—hope for a messiah still to come, hope for a
resolution to the human problem that God would bring, not as a capricious
deus ex machina but as the fulfillment of the work of redemption in which
God had already been engaged throughout Israel's history. Jews, then, can
look ahead, waiting in hope, in the light of what they have already seen and
already know of God's revelation. It is in the light of Exodus-Sinai, wherein
God is revealed as Israel's deliverer, that Israel looks forward to a more
ultimate deliverance that God will effect through the coming of the Messiah.
Different Jews anticipate this coming in different ways, to be sure, but all
share this waiting in hope, since the nature of the hope has been revealed:
"Wait *for the Lord!*" (In chapter 5 we will see another Jew, Elie Wiesel,
struggling with the fact that nothing, not even the Holocaust, seems sufficient
to move God to bring this hope to fruition in a suffering world.)

The fundamental difference, of course, between Judaism and Christianity is
that Christianity claims that the event for which Judaism still waits has already
taken place, a contrast we will develop more fully when looking at Elie Wiesel.
Martin Buber has helped to sharpen the contrast by declaring that to Christians,
Jews are stubborn people still waiting for a messiah; while to Jews, Christians
are heedless people who think that in an unredeemed world redemption has
already happened. But this "stumbling block to Jews" is likewise "foolishness to
Greeks," as Saint Paul acknowledged, and Buber's indictment is one that many
non-Jews, such as Nietzsche, lay at the door of Christianity itself. For the
ostensibly redeemed world does not look very redeemed, nor do the lives of the
redeemed exhibit the radical difference such a claim should make.

There is still a sense, however, in which Christians and Jews share a similar
posture; both look back, both look ahead, and both wait in hope. Each sees a
past disclosure of ultimate meaning; for the Jew it is Exodus-Sinai, for the
Christian it is Good Friday–Easter. Each looks toward a more complete
disclosure of that meaning; for the Jew it is the coming of the Messiah, for the
Christian it is the *eschaton,* the consummation of all things.

The decisive Christian claim is that the nature of ultimate reality has been
manifested *under the conditions of temporality;* the power of God has been
manifested in the weakness of a human being; the life of divine love has shown
itself in a life of human love. In short, "the Word [the creative power of God]

has become flesh and dwelt among us." That for which humanity waits has been defined in discernibly human terms, the terms of a human life and death, for which the only adequately descriptive word is love.

Waiting in Hope

With this background we can turn to W. H. Auden's poem *For the Time Being*, since it serves as a significant contrast to *Waiting for Godot*, *The Trial*, and *The Castle*. The poem is not a disguised Christian sermon but a work of creative art by a creative artist who happens to be a Christian, and in this instance happens to be writing about Christian subject matter. Auden is one of the few "Christian writers" in whose hands a Christian affirmation does not become saccharine. The poem makes demands on the reader because the author does not disavow the use of Christian imagery, but the demands are worth the effort since the poem illumines both the time of the Incarnation and our contemporary time.

When one waits in hope, in the light of the Incarnation, Auden indicates that at least three things can happen:

1. Waiting in hope makes possible a *radical honesty about the present*. No longer are rose-colored glasses necessary to keep us buoyed up, nor do analyses of despair represent the only possible approach to life. Easy optimism and easy pessimism are both undercut. Our fears can be openly expressed. Auden's Chorus can be just as "realistic" as the creations of a Beckett or a Kafka:

> Alone, alone about a dreadful wood
> Of conscious evil runs a lost mankind,
> Dreading to find its Father lest it find
> The Goodness it has dreaded is not good:
> Alone, alone about our dreadful wood.

Since, as the Chorus goes on to explain, "The Pilgrim Way has led to the Abyss," there is no longer any hope in human terms alone, and the alternatives of judgment or grace seem once again, though in a way subtly different from Kafka's, to be the true alternatives:

> We who must die demand a miracle.
> How could the Eternal do a temporal act,
> The Infinite become a finite fact?
> Nothing can save us that is possible:
> We who must die demand a miracle.

2. Waiting in hope makes possible *a radical honesty about the nature of the deliverance*. If it is true that there can be no schemes of self-deliverance (and on this Beckett and Kafka and Auden agree), then if there is salvation it will be of divine rather than human origin. The stakes are high in such a claim, for this is either sheer folly or what Paul called "the folly of God [that is] wiser than human wisdom." As Gabriel says to Mary,

> Love wills your dreams to happen, so
> Love's will on earth may be, through you,
> No longer a pretend but true.

Pretense or truth. . . . Along with Joseph, who is asked to believe what are to him preposterous claims about a virgin birth, the reader resists such monumental stakes and the terms on which they seem to be offered. Surely we can demand more evidence than is provided! Joseph's doubts become our doubts and he speaks for us:

> All I ask is one
> Important and elegant proof
> That what my love had done
> Was really at your will
> And that your will is Love.

To which Gabriel replies, "No, you must believe."

The mood of the Shepherds, before the angel appears, seems similar to that of Gogo and Didi: "What is real / About us all is that each of us is waiting," although Gogo and Didi are not always sure they are "real." The Shepherds' conversations, like the conversations of Gogo and Didi, are "mainly to keep us / From watching the clock all the time." The Shepherds know something will happen, but they do not know what. They are sure, however, that "one day or / The next we shall hear the Good News," which becomes the point at which their mood parts company with that of Gogo and Didi. In the Shepherds' case, "Godot" comes; the Shepherds are told that "A Son is given . . . proclaiming the ingression of Love." And as the Shepherds respond with the cry, "Let us run to Love," they learn that "The Father Abyss / Is affectionate / To all Its creatures."

To the non-Christian this sounds like sheer escapism, as though the cost of waiting in hope was paid in the coin of a retreat from the reality of the here and now. But the whole point is that meaning has *not* been found by "retreat" from the here and now; meaning has invaded the here and now, and confronted humanity in the midst of the daily routine—tending sheep in this particular instance. The conclusion of the "Meditation of Simeon" portrays the nature of the new situation:

And because of His visitation, we may no longer desire God as if He were lacking: our redemption is no longer a question of pursuit but of surrender to Him who is always and everywhere present. Therefore at every moment we pray that, following Him, we may depart from our anxiety into His peace.

3. Waiting in hope makes possible a *radical honesty about the resultant nature of the human situation.* The one who waits in hope does not confront a different world, but sees the same world in a different light. There is no justification for retreating from the world, for it is precisely *in the world* that meaning has become manifest. Indeed, the one who now relies on God must exhibit deep concern for the world that God has visited. The Chorus prays:

> Inflict Thy promises with each
> Occasion of distress,
> That from our incoherence we
> May learn to put our trust in Thee,
> And brutal fact persuade us to
> Adventure, Art, and Peace.

The nature of the human situation is not that distress, trial, and disappointment have now been erased. Indeed, as the Narrator points out in the powerful closing speech:

> To those who have seen
> The Child, however dimly, however
> Incredulously,
> The time being is, in a sense, the most trying time
> of all.

But since the stable, where all of this occurred, was planted firmly in the midst of this world, the place "where for once in our lives / Everything became a You and nothing was an It," a task is laid on all those who have visited the stable, a task expressed by the dialectic of waiting and working:

> In the meantime
> There are bills to be paid, machines to keep in repair,
> Irregular verbs to learn, the Time Being to redeem
> From insignificance.

This may not sound like much, but it is the promise of everything. For "the time being" is not to be written off, or grimly avoided, or even grimly accepted; it is to be "redeemed," to be "bought back" from insignificance, because it was in "the time being" that everything was transformed from an It to a You.

So the mood of one who waits in hope is a mood of affirmation. Even "the time being" can be an occasion for joy; the created order can be gladly affirmed because the Creator has appeared within it and sanctified all that has been made.

> He is the Life.
> Love Him in the World of the Flesh;
> And at your marriage all its occasions shall dance for joy.

The distance from Kafka to Auden is the distance from the concluding lines of *The Trial* to the concluding lines of *For the Time Being:* from "Like a dog!" to "dance for joy."

To no more than a minority in our day is the vision Auden proclaims a vision that can be believed. Those who would like it to be true often fear that it is not. Those who actively disbelieve it feel that its acceptance would be tantamount to an act of moral cowardice. But whether we cast our lot with Beckett or Kafka or Auden, whether we wait in doubt or dread or hope, we share with the others the essential fact that all of us are waiting. Auden would affirm that we share in the possession of something more. For, to let Paul Tillich have the last as well as the first word:

> Although waiting is *not* having, it is also having. The fact that we wait for something shows that in some way we already possess it. Waiting anticipates that which is not yet real. If we wait in hope and patience, the power of that for which we wait is already effective within us. He who waits in an ultimate sense is not far from that for which he waits. He who waits in absolute seriousness is already grasped by that for which he waits. He who waits in patience has already received the power of that for which he waits. He who waits passionately is already an active power himself, the greatest power of transformation in personal and historical life.

II

4

STRANGE NAMES FOR A SHAPELESS GOD
Ignazio Silone

If it were in my power to change the mercantile laws of literary society, I might well spend my life perpetually writing and rewriting the same story in the hope of at last understanding it and making it understood, just as in the Middle Ages there were monks who spent their whole lives painting and repainting the Saviour's face, always the same face, yet always different.
—Ignazio Silone, "Note on the Revision of Fontamara"

A first reading of Ignazio Silone's works might leave the impression that he is "dated." He is writing about the struggle of Italian peasants against fascism in the 1930s and about the lure of communism during that period as a possible alternative to the totalitarian status quo. It could be argued that his works are no more than an interesting series of canvases depicting what life was like in a historical and geographical setting now remote from us.

But to whatever degree Silone's works were hammered out on the anvil of concern for the downtrodden and oppressed, and to whatever degree they rose out of particular challenges presented by fascism and communism, their author has rightly seen that the story of the human spirit, threatened but not overcome during that period, is the story of the human spirit, threatened but not overcome, during every period.

Although his novels as originally written stand on their own even today, Silone employed the unusual device of rewriting a number of them, excising material that tied them too closely to the period of their origin, in order that the perennial concerns with which they deal could stand out in bolder relief. This he did with *Fontamara* (1934, 1960), *Bread and Wine* (1937, 1962), *The School for Dictators* (1938, 1963), and *The Seed Beneath the Snow* (1942, 1965).

Whether the device is always successful or not, the revised novels do force ongoing questions on the reader, and the events of the 1930s assume a disturbing relevance in relation to the events of the 1990s. Each book becomes a parable of contemporary human concerns. The parallels between the Italian "liberation" of Ethiopia and the American "liberation" of Vietnam, Grenada, Panama, and Kuwait are disturbing; the indictment of the indifference of the Italian church in the 1930s becomes an indictment of the indifference of the American church in the 1990s, and the disillusionment of various revolutionaries in Silone's novels foreshadows the problems with which both contemporary "leftists" and "neoconservatives" are having to come to grips.

The story Silone tells is, as he says, "the same story"—a story that needs retelling in each generation in terms understandable to that generation. It is a story often told without explicit reference to the word "God," but a story that is always grappling with what that word has meant for humanity, and what the reality to which it points might still mean. Silone, deeply steeped in a Christian faith he formally or at least institutionally rejected, found it impossible to deal with the deepest needs of the human spirit without employing the imagery of Christian faith and Christian history.

It is hard for anyone of sensitive conscience to affirm God's presence in the kind of world Silone depicts, so gross are the inequities between persons, so brutal is the destruction of human values, either by nature (using impersonal power) or by persons (using power impersonally). And yet if God is absent, that absence is a kind of creative absence, almost a brooding presence, the presence of a God seemingly at the mercy of the world; a God whose visitation of this tortured planet has forced God into hiding; a God who, when wishing to assert the divine presence, must employ pseudonyms—other names—in order to communicate a healing word. That Silone has faith in a God not dead but hidden, a God found (when found) in unlikely places, is surely a central fact in that "same story" Silone continues "writing and rewriting."

Formative Events in Silone's Life

Dangerous though it is to use the events of an author's life as a means of understanding his or her works, the device is helpful in Silone's case, since his own pilgrimage is close to that of many of the characters in his novels.

The terrible injustices of life around him were borne in upon Silone at an early age, as he recounts in an episode the reader might imagine to have come from one of his novels:

> I was a child just five years old when, one Sunday, while crossing the little square of my native village with my mother leading me by the hand, I witnessed the cruel, stupid spectacle of one of the local gentry setting his great dog at a poor woman, a seamstress, who was just coming out of church. The wretched woman was flung to the ground, badly mauled, and her dress was torn to ribbons. Indignation in the village was general, but silent. I have never understood how the poor woman ever got the unhappy idea of taking proceedings against the squire; but the only result was to add a mockery of justice to the harm already done. Although, I must repeat, everybody pitied her and many people helped her secretly, the unfortunate woman could not find a single witness prepared to give evidence before the magistrate, nor a lawyer to conduct the prosecution. On the other hand, the squire's supposedly Left-Wing lawyer turned up punctually, and so did a number of bribed witnesses, who perjured themselves by giving a grotesque version of what had happened, and accusing the woman of having provoked the dog. The magistrate—a most worthy, honest person in private life—acquitted the squire and condemned the poor woman to pay the costs.[1]

It became clear to Silone that attempts to combat such gross miscarriages of justice were not going to be effective through ordinary political means, since the whole system was rigged against the peasants. He describes the decision of the large landowner, "the Prince," to run for public office:

> The Prince was deigning to solicit "his" families for their vote so that he could become their deputy in parliament. The agents of the estate, who were working for the Prince, talked in impeccably liberal phrases: "Naturally," said they, "naturally, no one will be forced to vote for the Prince, that's understood; in the same way that no one, naturally, can force the Prince to allow people who don't vote for him to work on his land. This is the period of real liberty for everybody; you're free, and so is the Prince."[2]

The church played no role in the struggle, except to condone by its silence the activities of the landlords against the peasants. Its priests were indifferent to the peasants' fight for justice, and anxious to support the status quo. Silone recalls seeing a puppet show in which the devil marionette asked the children of the village where the child in the show was hiding. The children instinctively lied to save the child from the devil.

> Our parish priest, a most worthy, cultured and pious person, was not altogether pleased. We had told a lie, he warned us with a worried look. We had told it for good ends, of course, but still it remained a lie. One must never tell lies. "Not even to the devil?" we asked in surprise. "A lie is always a sin," the priest replied. "Even to the magistrate?" asked one of the boys. The priest rebuked him severely. "I'm here to teach you Christian doctrine and not to talk nonsense. *What happens outside the church is no concern of mine.*"[3]

Faced by injustice and dismayed by the impotence he felt at trying to bring about change through ordinary political means or through the church, Silone joined the Communist party. He was a member for many years. But disillusionment with the party came too, in terms described later in this chapter by Uliva, the disillusioned revolutionary of *Bread and Wine*. For Silone, and for Uliva, communism was indeed (in the title of the symposium from which the above excerpts are taken) "the god that failed." An act of faith had been made, an allegiance had been manifested, a commitment had been offered, and the god to whom the faith, the allegiance, and the commitment were made turned out to be a false god, an idol, a human creation rather than a deity worth living for and dying for.

Silone finally left the party. He did not become a cynic, however, and after his departure he could still voice a positive credo that had been won at the cost of many scars:

> My faith in Socialism (to which I think I can say my entire life bears testimony) has remained more alive than ever in me. In its essence it has gone back to what it was when I first revolted against the old social order; a refusal to admit the existence of destiny, an extension of the ethical impulse from the restricted individual and family sphere to the whole domain of human activity, a need for effective brotherhood, an affirmation of the superiority of the human person over all the economic and social mechanisms which oppress him. As the years have gone by, there has been added to this an intuition of man's dignity and a feeling of reverence for that which in man is always trying to outdistance itself, and lies at the root of his eternal disquiet.[4]

Where God Is and Is Not:
Five Interrelated Themes

Where is God in this political tangle? Where, in the novels written out of this experience, can one look for the divine reality? How does God relate to Silone's "intuition" of our dignity, to his "feeling of reverence" for that which in us "is always trying to outdistance itself," and to our "eternal disquiet"? It will not do to try to make an orthodox Christian out of Silone, but as we shall see, he draws heavily on orthodox and biblical imagery in dealing with the brooding presence of the divine. A description of five interrelated themes may help us to see how the "shapeless god" takes shape in Silone's writings.

1. One might initially expect that God would be found within the institution that exists to give God honor and praise, and that the church would be the abode of God's human dwelling. But the church, if it once gave witness

to a Master who came not to be served but to serve, seemingly does so no more. So there is in Silone's fiction *a strong critique of the church*. Don Benedetto, a priest in *Bread and Wine* who has been removed from his post because of his "advanced" ideas, suggests to a colleague that the church should condemn Mussolini's war against Ethiopia. Don Angelo, a conservative priest, recounts the conversation to Don Paolo:

> I replied, "But do you realize what would happen if the Church openly condemned the present war? What persecutions would descend upon it, and what moral and material damage would result." You will never imagine what Don Benedetto replied. "My dear Don Angelo," he said, "can you imagine John the Baptist offering Herod a concordat to avoid having his head cut off? Can you imagine Jesus offering Pontius Pilate a concordat to avoid the crucifixion?"
>
> 'That reply does not seem to me to be anti-Christian,' Don Paolo said.
>
> 'But the Church is not an abstract society,' Don Angelo said, raising his voice. 'The Church is what it is. It has a history of nearly 2,000 years behind it. It is no longer a young lady who can permit herself acts of foolhardiness and indiscretion. She is an old, a very old, lady full of dignity, respect, traditions, bound by rights and duties. It was of course founded by the crucified Jesus, but after him there came the apostles, followed by generations and generations of saints and popes. The Church is no longer a small, clandestine sect in the catacombs, but has a following of millions and millions of human beings who look to it for protection.'[5]

But it is not only the far-off war against Ethiopia that the church will not condemn. There is another war nearer at hand, the war against injustice and poverty, with which the church likewise refuses to involve itself. The story of this futile war is told poignantly in *Fontamara*, Silone's earliest novel. The peasants are tricked out of their water rights. The workers are tricked out of their pay by hidden taxes that become visible too late. When a movement of protest is finally launched, the town is pillaged, the women are raped, and the whole of Fontamara is destroyed. The book ends with the despairing cry:

> What are we to do?
> After so much anguish and so much mourning, so many tears and so many tricks, so much hate and injustice and despair, what are we to do?[6]

What they can do is what the narrators of *Fontamara* did—they can join the revolutionary forces.

What they cannot do is look to the church for help. The indictment of the church for its silence is epitomized by the dream of Zompa early in the book. The Pope and the Crucifix have a little talk. The Crucifix suggests all sorts of things the Pope could do for the people: the land could be given to them, for example. The Pope counters that the Prince wouldn't have it, and the Prince is a good Christian. Christ then suggests that the peasants could be exonerated from their taxes; the Pope replies that the government officials couldn't think of that, and they are good Christians too. In response to the suggestion that the peasants be sent a good crop, the Pope replies that if there is a good crop, prices will go down and the merchants will be ruined; and the merchants are likewise good Christians. Finally Christ and the Pope visit the villages, with Christ carrying a knapsack from which the Pope can take anything that will do the peasants some good:

> "In every village the Holy Visitors saw the same thing, and what else was there for them to see? The *cafoni* were grumbling, cursing, squabbling, and worrying, not knowing which way to turn for food or clothing. And the Pope was afflicted in his heart at what he saw. So he took from the bag a whole cloud of a new kind of lice and released them over the houses of the poor saying, 'Take them, my beloved children, and scratch yourselves. Thus, in your moments of idleness you will have something to distract your thoughts from sin.' "[7]

In *Bread and Wine,* another priest, Don Piccirelli, writes a paper on "The Scourge of Our Times." Don Benedetto asks him hopefully, "Have you written about war or unemployment?"

> 'Those are political issues,' Don Piccirilli replied drily. 'The diocesan journal deals only with religious questions. From the purely spiritual point of view the scourge of our time, in my opinion, is immodesty in dress.[8]

So much for the church's contribution to the social ills of humanity. It is no wonder that Rocco, in *A Handful of Blackberries,* gets up one day in the middle of mass and leaves the church, never to return. He suddenly realizes that those present are neither hot nor cold, and that God will spew them out of his mouth. Rocco chooses the poor as his comrades and makes his way into the Communist party, so he can work for the social justice he has found the church ignoring. If God is a God who cares for those whom God has created, it is clear that the institution perpetuating God's name has desecrated that name beyond redemption.

2. Where then is God found? Perhaps the God who appears to have been deserted by the church may be working in hiding elsewhere. The possibility brings us to the heart of Silone's theme, his conviction that *God's work is carried on through pseudonyms*.

Don Benedetto, the elderly priest in *Bread and Wine,* makes the point most directly, asserting that when things are not going well, and secrecy and conspiracy are the order of the day, God must sometimes hide and appear under strange guises and with strange names, or pseudonyms. God, Don Benedetto feels, is not very concerned about the words used to describe divine reality. It may even be the case that stirrings about social justice, present among ordinary people, represent one of the strange names God is using to escape from the control of the churches and the banks.[9]

Lest this seem too new an idea, too unorthodox in its simplications, Don Benedetto makes clear in a conversation with his former student Pietro Spina, now a revolutionary, that it has a long history:

> 'It would not be the first time that the Lord has been forced to hide Himself and make use of an assumed name. As you know, He has never attached much importance to the names men have given Him; on the contrary, one of the first of His commandments is not to take His name in vain. And sacred history is full of examples of clandestine living. Have you ever considered the meaning of the flight into Egypt? And later, when He had grown up, did not Jesus several times have to hide himself to escape from the Pharisees?'[10]

Don Benedetto also recalls the story of Elijah's encounter with God (1 Kings 19:9–13). God was not present in the wind or the earthquake or the fire—the accustomed signs of divine theophany in those times. God was present, unexpectedly, in a sound of soft stillness. So too today, God may not be present in open and public ways, but rather in quiet, hidden, unexpected deeds, in the pseudonymous activity of humble people. Reflecting on the Elijah story, Don Benedetto continues, describing certain actions in which he knows his listener to have been involved:

> 'I too in the depth of my affliction have asked, where then is the Lord and why has He abandoned us? The loudspeakers and the bells that announced the beginning of new butchery to the whole country were certainly not the voice of the Lord. Nor are the shelling and bombing of Abyssinian villages that are reported daily in the press. But if a poor man alone in a hostile village gets up at night and scrawls with a piece of charcoal or paints "Down with the war" on the walls the Lord is undoubtedly present. How is it possible not to see that behind that unarmed man in his contempt for danger, in his love of the so-called enemy, there is a direct reflection of the divine light? Thus, if simple workers are condemned by a special tribunal for similar reasons, there's no doubt about which side God is on.'[11]

The unexpectedness of the divine activity, the fact that God may choose to work through pseudonyms is, as Don Benedetto acknowledges, a familiar theme in Jewish and Christian history, as we also saw in the second chapter of this book. The prophet Isaiah warned that in an ensuing battle between the Israelites and the Assyrians, the power of God would indeed be revealed— but the revelation would come not through the chosen people of Israel but through the pagans of Assyria. Assyria would be "the rod of God's anger," even though the king of Assyria had no idea that he was being so used.[12] Paul Tillich wrote of "the latent church," the unexpected instrument through which the divine may be manifested, and which may be quite different from the institutional church.[13] Pascal similarly puts great store by Isaiah's discussion of the hidden God: "Truly, thou art a God who hidest thyself."[14] God can raise up children of Abraham from the very stones at hand. Since the churches do not serve God, it may be that the revolutionary forces can, and Don Benedetto later says of Spina, "Socialism is his way of serving God."[15]

At different periods of history, God may employ different pseudonyms. During the particular period about which Silone is writing, when the grossest denial of God is the inequity between rich and poor, it can be expected that the manifestations of God's presence will be found not among the rich, not among the landlords, not among the heads of state, but among the peasants. It is therefore highly consistent that the Christ figures in Silone's novels are drawn from among the peasants or those who identify with the peasants. The theme is present in *Fontamara,* Silone's earliest novel. Berardo, one of the peasants who participates in the abortive uprising against the landlords, is taken to jail, where he gets to know "the Mystery Man," a man seeking to organize the peasants. Realizing how important it is for the Mystery Man to be at liberty, Berardo confesses to the crimes of which the Mystery Man has been charged, in order that the latter may be released. Berardo feels his own life can have a meaning if he dies not for himself but for someone else, and for a cause greater than himself. After Berardo's confession the authorities beat him up, and "eventually they dragged him back to the cell by his legs and shoulders like Christ when He was taken down from the cross."[16]

Berardo lays down his life for his friends, and his action finally galvanizes the peasants into action; they form a newspaper to give voice to their opposition to the landowners. They are crushed, as we saw earlier, for victory is not yet something that is promised by God—a theme to which we shall return.

3. Silone, after his espousal of the revolutionary cause, does not become uncritical in that espousal. God may indeed choose to work pseudonymously through the forces of revolution, and socialism may indeed be a way of serving God, but Silone sees clearly that *the revolutionary forces, like the church, may also become corrupted.* When they do, they deny the God they unknowingly have served. The disillusionment of the revolutionary in several of Silone's novels mirrors the disillusionment that emerged from his own years as a Communist.

The theme is stressed fictionally in *A Handful of Blackberries.* Rocco, who had walked out of church one day and joined the Communist party, makes the discovery that the Party of today is not what it once was. Having been a party of the oppressed, it has become a party of oppressors. So Rocco has to leave the party as well, and there remains for him only a life of lonely protest against all forms of corruption, a life spent as part of a remnant able to do little but wait for a day of deliverance that has not yet come.[17]

What has gone wrong? Why has the revolutionary cause fallen victim to the malady it was trying to correct? For what reason does it become increasingly difficult for Silone to identify God's pseudonyms with the forces of revolution?

Perhaps the clearest answer is that in concern for revolution on behalf of humanity, humanity itself becomes dehumanized, and must find a way back from impersonal ideology to a recovery of humanity. The progression of attitudes in Pietro Spina, whom we first meet as a revolutionary-in-hiding in *Bread and Wine*, is most instructive. At first Spina is simply one who organizes groups for resistance, rebellion, and possibly death. But as the book progresses, his enforced hiding (disguised as a priest) results in his beginning to enter into human relationships, to recover a feeling for *persons*, and to discover that these are more important than impersonal ideologies. He learns that one can find more human solidarity in shared humanity than in shared political convictions. Disguised as Don Paolo, Spina finds a young peasant named Infante, follows him home, and starts giving him a political lecture. Infante gives him food. Spina's landlady finally locates him in Infante's hut and urges him to return to the inn for dinner:

'I'm not hungry,' said Don Paolo. 'Go back to the inn, because I want to go on talking to this friend of mine.'

'Talking to him?' Matalena exclaimed. 'But haven't you noticed that the poor lad is a deaf-mute and only understands a few signs?'

The deaf-mute was sitting at the entrance to his den next to the priest. Don Paolo looked him in the face and saw realization of the mistake of which he had been the cause slowly dawning in his eyes.

'It doesn't matter,' the priest said to Matalena, 'go back to the inn, I'm not hungry.'

The two stayed where they were, and the one of them that had the gift of speech was silent too. Every so often they looked at each other and smiled. The grey light of evening faded and was followed by the darkness of night. As soon as it was dark torpor descended on the village almost immediately. But for the stench coming from the hovels and sheds the valley might have been uninhabited. After a time Don Paolo rose, shook the deaf-mute by the hand and wished him goodnight.[18]

This seemingly trivial episode has deep significance for Spina. His concerns shift more and more from ideological politics to human love. In the sequel to *Bread and Wine, The Seed Beneath the Snow*, Spina finally moves out of his own house and into the barn, sharing a stall with the deaf man, Infante. A remarkable bond is established between them. Spina taught Infante a new word, "brotherhood." Infante was already able to sound out "bread," which came out as *brod,* and with the help of gestures Spina communicated to him that when people share the same bread they are *brod-ers* or companions. "Brother" comes from *brod,* which stands for bread. Infante made the connection. By the very next day he was feeding bits of bread to the mice who shared their abode, and who ran across the straw on the lookout for bread crumbs. He accompanied the gesture by saying to Spina, *"Brod-ers."* From this point on, Infante began to offer bread to the donkey each day, so that the donkey could also be a brother.

This time in the stall was very important for Spina and did something important for his inner being. He felt that he had become a new person, stripped clean of what had been before. He was no longer an actor playing a part in the theater, uttering carefully rehearsed lines, but could truly be himself.[19]

For Spina, what goes on in the stable turns out to be far more important than would have seemed possible to the earlier revolutionary; it established a human relationship across seemingly impossible barriers. This kind of relationship becomes more important to Spina than anything else, and finally, at the end of the book, when Infante has killed his father, Spina takes responsibility for the deed, confesses to the crime he did not commit, and lays down his life for his friend.

In *The Secret of Luca,* Andrea Cipriani, a politician, returns to his native village to run for public office. He arrives just at the time that Luca, a simple peasant, is released from jail. Luca has spent a lifetime in jail for a crime he did not commit, and which the people of the village know he did not commit. They are frightened by his return, even though he seems to have no vengeance in his heart against those who could have demonstrated his innocence in court and failed to do so. Cipriani determines that he must discover the "secret" of Luca. What would motivate a man to let his life be destroyed in this way? Cipriani's attention is deflected more and more from his politicking, as he discovers in Luca a fierce and stubborn integrity that was willing to endure forty years of imprisonment to protect the honor of another individual.

There is a dimension of human understanding that politics does not reveal. This does not mean that politics becomes unimportant, but means only that politics needs, visionary as it may sound, to be infused by love. Without this ingredient, the most dedicated revolutionary will fall into the trap Uliva so convincingly sketches. The need is one that Rocco, both disillusioned churchman and disillusioned revolutionary, comes to sense. Rocco revises

Descartes' *Cogito ergo sum* (I think, therefore I am) to *Amo ergo sum* (I love, therefore I am). This, it will be noted, is very different from the formula of another famous revolutionary, Albert Camus, who declared, "I rebel, therefore we are." Perhaps the fullest statement of the principle would go even beyond Rocco, and emerge as *Amo ergo sumus* (I love, therefore we are), since love must leap the boundary from the self to other selves.

Silone thus captures the disillusionment into which revolutionaries can be led and recognizes the ingredient that must enter into the ethos of revolutionaries if they are to avoid being transmuted into replicas of that which they wish to overcome. That ingredient is love.

4. Once again, however, Silone does not fall victim of simplistic thinking. He offers no assurance that love will "win" or pay off. The one who loves does so at tremendous risk. And here again the theme of the pseudonyms of God comes to the forefront. For just as human love offers no assurance of success, neither does divine love. In the preface to *And He Did Hide Himself* (a stage version of *Bread and Wine*), Silone makes the point clearly: *"In the sacred history of man on earth, it is still, alas, Good Friday."* Those "who hunger and thirst after righteousness" are still derided, persecuted, put to death. The human spirit is still forced to save itself in hiding.[20] The message is that God has come to humanity, but humanity has not been willing to receive God. Humanity has, in fact, rejected God. God is present, not as triumphant presence but as brooding presence, as suffering presence, a suffering into which those who "hunger and thirst after righteousness" can expect to be initiated. In the play, Silone introduces Brother Giocchino, a wandering friar, who has been expelled from his order for giving voice to the dangerous notion that Christ has not risen, that God is still in hiding, that it is still Good Friday. Brother Giocchino points out that certain people have become disillusioned because they believe that God is no longer on earth. It is Brother Giocchino's belief, however, that God is *still* on earth; hiding, to be sure, and certainly in agony, but still here. And as long as He is still here, and not dead, despair is not allowed. It may even be that those on earth are given the task of seeing that He does not die.[21]

The theme is not incidental to Silone, and he introduces it again in *Seed Beneath the Snow*, the sequel to *Bread and Wine*. Don Marcantonio reminds a carpenter, Master Eutimio, that Jesus isn't on the cross any more. But Master Eutimio responds seriously that some people believe that Jesus is still on the cross, that He has not yet died or ascended into heaven. If he is still dying on earth, it would explain a great deal.[22] The very symbolism of the book's title reinforces the point. The seed has indeed been planted, but it is still "the seed beneath the snow," the seed that has not yet come to flower. Furthermore, the action of the book takes place during Lent. Both facts suggest a theme of anticipation but not of fulfillment. The theme is reminiscent, as are so many of Silone's themes, of Pascal, who exclaims in the *Pensées*, "Jesus will be in agony even to the end of the world."[23]

That Christ has come to earth and has been crucified is, of course, part of the central Christian story. It is not the whole of that story, which includes the claim that Christ's death was not the end of the story, and that only in the light of his resurrection from the dead can one really bear the full burden of the message of the cross. There is, however, a Christian sentimentalism that leaps too quickly over Good Friday to Easter Sunday, that seeks victory without defeat, and triumph without tragedy. It does not understand the meaning of servanthood and suffering servanthood. In the face of such one-sided claims, Silone's counterclaim, that it is still Good Friday and that Easter has not come, is an important one. No victory worth having is ever cheaply won. Silone, however, refuses to let the unabated optimism of an Easter without Good Friday be transformed into the utter pessimism of a Good Friday without an Easter. For while he says that Easter has not come, he does not say that it cannot come. One can continue to hope, as Brother Giocchino and Master Eutimio do, and as all may, but one must not allow such hope to be falsely and prematurely claimed. There is a sober realism here that is clearly appropriated from the Gospels, even though Silone is unable to make the full affirmation that the Gospels make. While humanity must wait—a theme we explored in the preceding chapter—humanity nevertheless waits with a certain hope, having seen in anticipation what will one day be realized fully.

5. The above themes converge in a way that summarizes Silone's concern with God's strange names. If God cannot be seen clearly and distinctly but is still hidden by pseudonyms, and it is still Good Friday, there are at least certain events that help to reveal God. *Earthly events can image divine events,* a theme we shall encounter in the writings of Charles Williams as well. That which we experience in utterly human terms can contain portents of the hidden God. We have already seen that the death of Berardo was more than the death of a peasant. It was a contemporary reenactment of the death of Christ, a way of dramatizing in contemporary terms Jesus' statement, "Greater love hath no man than this, that a man lay down his life for his friends."

Luigi Murica, in *Bread and Wine,* is another peasant whose death points to much more than appears on the surface. When word is received of Murica's death in Rome, dying for another, friends gather at his parents' home. They sit around the table. The elder Murica gives them food and drink, and the parallel to the Holy Eucharist, now being enacted in a simple peasant hut, is apparent.

> 'He helped me to sow, hoe, reap, thresh and grind the corn of which this bread is made. Take it and eat, this is his bread.'
> Others arrived. The father poured out wine and said, 'He helped me to prune, spray, hoe, and gather the grapes of the vineyard from which this wine came. Drink, for this is his wine.'[24]

A little later in the meal, Spina comments:

> 'Bread is made of many grains of corn,' said Pietro, 'so it means unity. Wine is made of many grapes, so it means unity too. Unity of similar, equal, useful things. Hence truth and fraternity are also things that go well together.'
> 'The bread and wine of Holy Communion,' an older man said. 'The wheat and the grapes that are trampled on. The body and the blood.'[25]

The double meaning of this episode, from which the title *Bread and Wine* is derived, is apparent. Bread and wine are necessities of life, imperative for sheer physical survival, and they thus stand for food and drink. But bread and wine stand for more than food and drink. Bread, as we have already seen, stands for companionship, for companions (*cum-panis*) are those who share their bread; and the bread and wine together, as Spina testifies, stand for unity, and thus for truth and human companionship.

Silone, however, goes beyond such levels as these, for his account of the meal in the home of Luigi Murica's parents is (as we have seen) shot through with allusions to the holy meal of Jesus and his disciples. It is not only the meal consumed at the altar in the church that is a holy meal; *any* meal, even in the rudest peasant's house, can be holy—a showing forth of the divine through earthy vehicles. Murica's body has been broken, and Murica's blood has been shed, on behalf of the victims of injustice, in the name of truth and human companionship. And since he threshed the grain and trod the grapes, the bread and the wine are indeed "his" bread and "his" wine. And Murica, when he lays down his life for his friends, witnesses both to the integrity of his own deed and to the ongoing presence of the hidden God who has adopted the pseudonym of a suffering humanity.

In those moments when one person suffers for another, he or she gives shape to the "shapeless god" and makes clear that God, too, participates in suffering so endured. Silone affirms that the material can be the vehicle of the spiritual, and his way of doing so destroys the propriety of such a mode of speaking, for he is really saying that the material and the spiritual are indivisible, and that a person who truly comprehends the one likewise comprehends the other. If it is unlikely that God should be present in a peasant's hut when eating and drinking are taking place, it is just as unlikely that God should have been present in a Palestinian peasant's hut as the son of a village carpenter. God may be unexpected in either place, but God's presence having been discerned in one place lends credence to that presence in other places as well. Every table can be holy, every meal a eucharist, every deed of love a revelation.

Silone's world is a world unfinished. It has been confronted by the presence of God, and being unable to bear that presence, has tried to destroy it. It has not succeeded in destroying that presence, although it has succeeded in forcing the divine into hiding, into the adoption of pseudonyms. But the divine continues to call upon us to discover God in most unlikely places—in the man who writes in chalk "Down with the war," in the peasant who confesses to the crimes of another, in the revolutionary who teaches a deaf man the meaning of companionship—and thereby to assist God in the work of bringing creation to completion. It is a strange, hidden, shapeless, pseudonymous God, this God of Silone. But if we miss God's presence in the world, perhaps it is not because God is not there, but simply because we have been looking in the wrong places.

5

THE HUMAN OBLIGATION TO QUESTION GOD
Elie Wiesel

In *Legends of Our Time,* Elie Wiesel writes, "Words can sometimes, in moments of grace, attain the quality of deeds." The Nobel Prize Committee made an appropriate commentary on that remark in 1985 by awarding the Nobel Peace Prize to Wiesel, survivor of Auschwitz, novelist, essayist, playwright, man of letters, and teacher, whose words have carved themselves on the hearts and consciences of millions of people through the more than thirty books he has written over thirty years. It is significant that the prize was not for literature but for peace. Great writer though he is, Wiesel is also a peacemaker, one whose words do, in his own life, "attain the quality of deeds."

Wiesel insists that he is not a political person; he does not stump for candidates, engage in party politics, or follow an ideological line. And yet on another level he is one of the most political people of our time: everything he does flows from his conviction that all persons are worthy of infinite respect. *All* persons, not just Jews, not just survivors of the death camps, but all persons, starting especially with victims, whether in South Africa, the Sohel, Bangladesh, Cambodia, or Russia—places where Wiesel has himself gone to carry a message of solidarity and hope.

One of the most creative "political" acts of our time was Wiesel's fervent plea to President Reagan, before millions of television viewers, not to visit the Bitburg Cemetery in Germany and so honor the S.S. troops buried there—an embodiment of "speaking truth to power." And although power chose not to listen, millions were fortified to discover that the words and deeds of the prophets were alive and well in our time.

Words and deeds are one for Elie Wiesel. In reading his books one discovers the moral passion out of which he is driven to be a witness to, and a messenger of, the Holocaust—a constant reminder that the horror must never happen again, to anyone. His passion includes anger but never hatred. For though we must be angry at injustice, we must not hate, not even the doers of injustice, lest we become like them and thus give them the final victory.

Wiesel has his quarrels with human iniquity, and also his quarrels with God. He insists that engagement with God, both pleading with God and challenging God on moral grounds, is part of our task as human beings. Our shouts and our anger, even against God, are appropriate. In such situations, as one of Wiesel's characters in *The Town Beyond the Wall* informs us, our shouts and even our blasphemies are a form of prayer. They indicate that we are taking God seriously. And when we take God that seriously, we find that we have to take God's creatures seriously too.

It works both ways: it is partly because we must take God's creatures seriously that we have to take God seriously as well, difficult as that is in a world that seems either devoid of the presence of a loving God, or filled with examples of a malevolent God. We will explore two treatments of this intermingling of concern for God and God's creatures, Wiesel's recasting of an ancient Jewish tale of pressing human questions on God to the nth degree, and an example of the same exercise in contemporary terms.

Ani Maamin: A Song Lost and Found Again

The mystery of the coming of a messiah, a deliverer sent from God, demonstrating that history moves toward a fulfillment, is a mystery Jews and Christians share, even though they stand on opposing sides of a great divide in their interpretation of the hope to which that mystery points.

In an important essay, "The Two Foci of the Jewish Soul," Martin Buber describes the ultimate division between Judaism and Christianity messianically, but he also suggests that our point of deepest division is the area in which we have the most in common. What we have in common, he writes, is "a book and an expectation." To the Christian the book is a forecourt, to the Jew it is the sanctuary. But, he goes on, "In this place we can dwell together, and together listen to the voice that speaks here." The Christian's expectation, he says, "is directed toward a second coming, ours to a coming which has not been anticipated by a first." But, he continues, "we can wait for the advent of the One together, and there are moments when we may prepare the way before him together."

Buber states realistically that "Pre-messianically our destinies are divided. Now to the Christian the Jew is the incomprehensibly obdurate man, who declines to see what has happened; and to the Jew the Christian is the incomprehensibly daring man, who affirms in an unredeemed world that its redemption has been accomplished." Even in this division, Buber concludes, we can engage in a common watch, holding fast to our own separate faiths, but caring "more for God himself than for our images of God."

It is in this spirit that Christians must approach, with profound gratitude, the throbbing, despairing, and yet strangely hopeful song that Elie Wiesel has recovered from his Hasidic childhood and sung again in *Ani Maamin*. It is an old song, a song about the Messiah and his failure to appear—a probing that is by turns insistent, pleading, tearful, strident, despairing, and yet finally full of hope, both veiled and visible, that can, in spite of all the horror and heartache, enable us to face the future.

The Messianic coming, as Buber intimates, poses different problems for Christians and Jews, and part of the Jewish contribution to Christian Messianism is a reminder that a claim that the Messiah has come is as much a problem as a solution. The problem, of course, is that if the Messianic hope has been fulfilled in Jesus of Nazareth, if redemption has occurred, evil nevertheless persists demonically in the "redeemed" world. What kind of messiah can Christians announce as "good news," when the world seems so unchanged by his advent and suffering persists unchecked? Better no messiah, it might be suggested, than such a one.

If that is not a real problem to Christians, then Christians need more than ever to hear the voice of Jews, who, as Buber reminds us, "experience, perhaps more intensely than any other part [of the world], the world's lack of redemption." If Christians have a problem that forces them to ask, "Why, if the Messiah has come, is the world so evil?" Jews also have a problem that forces them to ask, "Why, if the world is so evil, does the Messiah not come?" If God's children stand in such crushing need of deliverance, why is deliverance withheld? Can one, in such a world, have any hope for the future? Can one hope that even yet, at this late time, fulfillment and redemption will still come? Most poignant of all, may it not be the case that even if the Messiah comes, *he will come too late?*

With infinite variety, Wiesel presses the Messianic theme. The strands of hope are slender, and often virtually invisible, but there always remains a willingness to persist in asking the questions. For if we often seem to be "hope turned to dust," we are also, amazingly, "dust turned to hope." On occasion, most notably perhaps at the conclusion of *The Gates of the Forest*, a hope is expressed that the Messiah is not one person, but can and must be present in all persons, whose very presence in the world, singing, praying, crying, and obdurately questioning, is a sign that forsakenness is not the only word.

Ani Maamin is Wiesel's most poignant pressing of the Messianic question. It is the libretto of a cantata, set to music by Darius Milhaud. The writing is in blank verse, spare and taut, and its very economy of line contributes to the enormous anguish built up as the cumulative questions addressed to God assume an almost unbearable intensity. *Ani maamin beviat ha-Mashiah* is one of Maimonides' thirteen articles of faith: "I believe in the coming of the Messiah." Wiesel sang the song as a young Hasidic Jew in Transylvania, and believed it. Then he heard it sung in the death camps and wondered how it could be sung there. How could one "believe in the coming of the Messiah" during and after the Holocaust? So the song was "lost." Could it possibly be "found" again? The book is Wiesel's exploration of that possibility, focused in a tale.

The cantata retells an ancient story of Abraham, Isaac, and Jacob wandering the earth, only this time they are doing it during the era of the Holocaust. They return to the heavenly precincts to plead the cause of the Jews before God in this, their time of greatest tribulation. Each patriarch recounts a crucial event from his own past, Abraham as the first to affirm God as the Redeemer, Isaac as the one who faced his own sacrifice uncomplainingly, and Jacob as the one who dreamed of a ladder to earth from heaven. Each insists that God has abandoned the future promised to him and to his children, a future that has been turned to ashes. Jacob asks:

> You promised me to watch over Israel—
> Where are You? What of your promise?
> You promised me blessings for Israel—
> Is this your blessing?

The patriarchs weep. The angels weep. But God does not weep. God remains silent. Again Jacob implores him:

> Faithful God, behold the torment
> That bears your seal,
> As does the faith
> Of your victims.

The devastation continues, even as they speak. And with each Jewish death, another fragment of the Temple goes up in flames. Hope is being murdered as never before. But from the celestial tribunal, only silence . . .

The pleaders intensify their urgency. Abraham did not know that the road from Ur to Canaan would end in Treblinka. Isaac did not know that the vision from Mount Moriah would include Majdanek. Jacob on his way to Bethel did not know

> That every road
> At dusk
> Would lead to Auschwitz.

Each gives an example of the utter destruction the Holocaust has brought: a bunker in Warsaw where a Jewish hand had to silence forever the cry of a Jewish child lest the hiding place be discovered, a death march in a forest where a father cannot console a son, a despairing suicide in a concentration camp. The Chorus supports the patriarchs and cries out to heaven: "Your children implore you: Hear and answer!" But heaven remains silent. . . .

A plea follows not only for those who have been slaughtered, but for those who have survived and feel guilty for surviving. There is an anguished question about a divine capriciousness that grants indulgence to executioners while chastisements are inflicted on children.

Finally, the silence of heaven is broken—not by God, but by an angel who comes to plead God's cause. We hear the familiar arguments offered in the book of Job: Who are you to question the divine power or plan? God has reasons. You are not to challenge but to accept. There will be salvation in the end.

But Abraham interrupts with the crucial question:

> You showed me messianic times—
> But what kind of messiah
> Is a messiah
> Who demands
> Six million dead
> Before he reveals himself?

The angel can only respond:

> God consoles.
> That is enough.

And at that, the pleading turns to anger. It is *not* enough! It can *never* be enough! Abraham, Isaac, and Jacob respond that they and their people will never be "consoled." It is impossible to be "consoled" for Belsen, or "rewarded" for Birkenau, or "forgetful" of Majdanek.

And so the patriarchs decide to leave heaven, their mission having failed. All they can do is return to earth and tell the people that there is no hope: "For now it is clear: God knows—and remains silent. God knows—so it must be his will." The executioners have won. The three patriarchs step back to leave, and God is still silent. . . .

Which would, of course, be a dramatic place to conclude. Who could blame Wiesel, or any Jew—or any person sensitive to the suffering of others—for concluding there? A plea has been made (*"Do* something. . . . Send the Messiah!") and the plea has been ignored.

But the song does not conclude. It goes on. Something new enters. The Chorus, which has been supportive of the patriarchs' outcry, ceases to echo the outcry and instead invokes blessing upon them. Blessing! If God will not provide a blessing, Israel will provide it. If God remains silent, Jews who have revered God's name will not.

Each of the patriarchs, as he withdraws from the heavenly throne, recounts a tale in which, in the face of unsurmountable odds and a silent heaven, a Jew nevertheless affirms. In one instance, a child expressed belief in the one who is carrying her, futilely, away from the Nazi machine guns. In another, a Jew in a doomed village suddenly "sings / of his ancient and lost faith," proclaiming that he still believes in the coming of the Messiah, even though the Messiah is late, even though God may be unwilling. In a third, a Jew in a death camp on the first night of Passover, unable to celebrate the meal, nevertheless can say:

> Still, I recite the Haggadah
> As though I believe in it.
> And I await the prophet Elijah,
> As I did long ago,

ending with the challenge to God:

> I shall wait for you.
> And even if you disappoint me
> I shall go on waiting.

"Auschwitz," he declares, "has killed Jews / But not their expectation."

After each of these recitals of an indomitable willingness to go on waiting, to refuse to succumb fully to despair, the Narrator informs us that God is being moved. After the first story, "a tear clouds his eyes," then "a tear streams down God's somber countenance," and finally, "God, surprised by his people, weeps for the third time—and this time without restraint, and with—yes—love." No one sees this weeping. It is veiled from the sight of Abraham, Isaac, and Jacob. But the faith of God's children has moved God deeply. "Moved" God, indeed, in the most literal sense of the word, for as Abraham, Isaac, and Jacob go away, the Narrator informs us that although they do not know it, "They are no longer alone: God accompanies them, weeping, smiling, whispering," as they return to the suffering earth. So finally God *does* speak, and "The word of God continues to be heard. So does the silence of his dead children."

God's presence is a veiled presence. No one knows of it. But there is another hope as well, suggested in each of the examples that finally moves God to a weeping and smiling engagement with God's people. This is the hope that Abraham, Isaac, and Jacob have in *their children,* and in the ongoing life of the Jewish community. Before the machine guns, the child bespoke faith; in the village, a Jew continued to believe; in the death camp an inmate affirmed that, even there, he would wait for the Messiah to come. These acts of human presence are *not* veiled. And it is out of such affirmation, of a presence and a hope both veiled and unveiled, that the story of God's people continues to be written.

Wiesel does not only write a song *about* hope for a future that lies in Israel's children. He places himself within the circle of hope by dedicating the book to his own son:

> For Shlomo-Elisha
> Son of Eliezer,
> Son of Shlomo,
> Son of Eliezer.

These are the first words one sees after the title page. They cannot really be read until after one has read the final page. Then they become a smile through tears.

Buber told us that "we can wait for the advent of the One together, and there are moments when we may prepare the way before him together." Wiesel in *Ani Maamin* makes his contribution to that preparing of the way. He has given us a creation of fearful beauty. He has found a lost song. He has sung it for us. If we are "to prepare the way . . . together," our own present task is, in the fullness of gratitude, to listen.

Madness, Caprice, Friendship, and God

Wiesel loves madmen. They people the pages of his novels with relentless consistency. This fascination with madness is not some voyeuristic desire on Wiesel's part to focus on crippled minds or bizarre deeds. On the contrary, it is part of his central concern to discover as much of the truth as we can discover. For it is his contention that madmen usually see the world more clearly than the so-called "sane," and that their judgments are consequently more trustworthy. If this is so, Wiesel should consider himself in good company, since, as one of his characters in *The Town Beyond the Wall* comments, "God loves madmen. They're the only ones he allows near him" (p.

24). Another character later picks up the refrain: "Since the beginning of history madmen have represented the divine presence" (p. 101).

Madness

In *Twilight*, a recent novel, Wiesel extends the logic of his concern for discerning the divine by giving us not only an occasional madman but a whole asylum full—inmates all of Mountain Clinic in upstate New York. They have an interesting trait in common: with one exception, they all think they are biblical characters: Adam, Cain, Abraham, Nadav son of Ahron, Joseph, the Messiah, even (in the closing climactic pages) a character who has assumed the role of God. In another part of the story Yoel Lipkin takes upon himself the mantle of Jeremiah. Just to round out the cycle, Raphael Lipkin, the protagonist in the novel, thinks he is probably going mad, too, and spends a considerable amount of time testing his hypothesis.

This might sound like a dismal theme even for serious readers, who probably have enough reminders of madness in their own daily lives not to need further reinforcement from the world of fiction. To those who think so, some countervailing factors should be noted.

One reason for the power of the book is that the madmen we encounter through the eyes of Raphael Lipkin are extraordinarily perspicacious, offering perspectives on the world and God that are not only original but profound. We can learn from them. This is particularly true of Abraham, if less so of the Messiah, who suffers under the existential handicap of being the son of a Protestant minister—an extremely clever theological riposte on Wiesel's part. We learn to sympathize with Cain and his overbearing father's preference for another sibling who may or may not exist, and, in the closing pages, to agonize with God, who carries an extremely heavy burden of responsibility, particularly when pinned to the dialogical mat by the relentless questioning of Raphael, whose entire family and closest friend were devoured by the behemoth called the Holocaust.

The most telling of these biblical characterizations is Adam, who devotes himself unremittingly to intercessory prayer. He has an unwavering agenda: he pleads night and day with God to call off the whole creation process immediately, since (as Adam can see with a prescience apparently denied to God) God peaked too early, and from the moment of creation things have been going downhill. "Countless souls who will escape the curse of being born only to die" (p. 39) will applaud such divine self-restraint, Adam tells God. So will the trees that men will never cut down and burn, along with the animals who will never be slaughtered and eaten. All of creation, in fact, will laud the putative Creator who "does not shrink from admitting His error," but has the chutzpah to close the book on creation before the first page has been turned. In a burst of generosity, Adam even offers to let God take credit for the proposal, content that it be perceived as having emanated from a divine rather than human source, so long as its content is honored.

If the portrayal of Adam is the most telling, the portrayal of Abraham is the most poignant. Jews (and all readers of the Bible) continually have to wrestle with the figure of Abraham, who is called upon by God to sacrifice his only son—a theme Wiesel has already dealt with powerfully in *Messengers of God*. How would this heaviest of all burdens have a counterpart in the lives of Jews hiding from the Nazis in World War II? Wiesel shows us a contemporary Abraham who is able to command the trust and loyalty of his son, and yet who, like his biblical counterpart, fills the son with illusions that turn out to be destructive.

While the modern Abraham and his son are in hiding, the father keeps transmitting the Jewish heritage to the son through study and yet more study. The non-Jewish peasant who is hiding them cannot understand: why all the attention to books? The son will only be able to survive by learning to outrun his pursuers, live on herbs, and pass as a Christian if captured. Abraham will have none of it. The power of the Word is everything, and the Word will protect them all.

But of course, as Abraham is later forced to acknowledge, "the Word did not save us" (p. 98). Many Jews were rounded up. A lot escaped because they could outrun their pursuers, live on herbs, and pass as Christians. But not Isaac. He had not been trained in survival skills, and Abraham feels—knows— that it was the father's fault the son did not survive.

Here a digression on madness is in order so that we do not miss the point. Wiesel distinguishes varying degrees, or levels, of madness. We all know about "clinical madness," infecting those who have lost all touch with reality. Out of extreme mental, moral, or psychic anguish, they inhabit an irrational private world in which they may routinely see elephants under toadstools, receive messages from Martians through dental fillings, or feel mandated to kill all redheads because God has told them to. Such people we isolate from society for their own protection and ours—particularly if we are redheads. This is not the kind of madness with which Wiesel is chiefly concerned, however, even though the madness about which he writes can also result in people being sent to asylums.

Wiesel, on the contrary, writes about what he sometimes calls "mystical madness," what Abraham Heschel called "the madness of the prophets," the madness of those who see life in such a different perspective from the rest of us that the rest of us become uneasy in their presence and seek to incarcerate them, or, if necessary, put them to death. The Hebrew prophets got this sort of treatment routinely from the defenders of the status quo, Jesus of Nazareth got it from the Romans, Archbishop Romero got it from the military, and six million Jews got it from the Nazis.

The threat of the "mystically mad" is this: they have such a different view of reality from ours that if we don't dispose of them we will have to listen to them and take them seriously. And if we did that, a gnawing feeling of unease might rise in us: *what if they are right and we are wrong?*

Such unease is not to be entertained. So, if annihilation is not a socially approved policy, we settle for incarceration, or at least ridicule, for calling them "mad" is sometimes sufficiently degrading to ostracize them from polite society.

So the threat of Wiesel's madmen is that they have a surer, saner corner on the truth than we do. A proposal: listen to the tales of the various biblical madmen that Raphael Lipkin interviews, and ask whether they may not be closer to the way things really are than their hearers.

Madness and Caprice

Another reason why the book does not pall in anticipation is that it contains plot threads in addition to the stories of life in an asylum for the mentally disturbed. The central thread in the overall tapestry is the story of the Lipkin family. It is not a happy story; indeed, it is an utterly tragic one, and anyone who survived it might, like Raphael Lipkin, always be fearful of going mad, mystically as well as clinically.

The Lipkin story is drenched in all the tangible horror of the "real world"—a world of invasions, battles, informers, rare moments of beauty, frequent moments of epidemics, cowardice, courage, refugees, heroic actions, and tragic miscalculations. It is the story of the annihilation of a Jewish family at the hand of the Nazis, a story Wiesel has told in many forms before, but never, perhaps, so sparsely or starkly as here.

The consistent theme in the story is caprice, and that is certainly a truth about the Holocaust we need to keep relearning. Yes, there was diabolical human design in the planning and carrying out of the Holocaust, but there was absolutely no logic that dictated why this person should survive and not that one; there was no relationsip between virtue and survival, or even between wisdom and survival. There was only caprice; a "safe" hiding place would be uncovered by the Nazis on the only day it was used; a brash act might (or, equally, might not) contribute to survival; an evasive action useful on one day would guarantee capture on the next or preceding day; a plan that worked for one family would, under identical outward circumstances, mutate into a trap sprung on another family. The Greeks had a phrase for all this:

Whirl is King, having overthrown Zeus. Holocaust version: Caprice reigns, having replaced Yahweh.

The story of the Lipkin family's inexorable dismemberment may be a compelling reason for madness, a justification for seeing the utter folly of the universe, and asserting, as several characters in the book assert, that the only "sensible" way to view the destruction is to posit that God too is mad, mad enough to let such things happen. In such a mood one could embrace the "sanity" of the mad Adam in suggesting that the whole venture of creation was at best (or at worst) a divine miscalculation, and, that once inaugurated, could not be (or at least was not) retrieved in time.

So the first and second stories—of the mad inmates and the vortex of the Holocaust—intersect more fully than might appear on an initial reading, and it is a matter of artistic skill to have interwoven them as skillfully as Wiesel does, by the device of having the sole survivor of the Lipkin family spend a summer interrogating the self-avowed biblical characters at the Mountain Clinic. Raphael visits there as a result of an impetus provided by his involvement in a third story, the story of Pedro, a story that holds together the apparently disparate stories of the inmates of the asylum and their visitor.

Caprice and Friendship

Pedro's story unfolds with tantalizing slowness. From the first page, there are italicized portions representing Raphael's interior dialogues with Pedro. It would not be fair to unmask too much of the Pedro story to those who have not read the book; and even if the attempt were made, it might be inaccurate, for Pedro is an enigmatic character, whose tracks Wiesel keeps pretty well covered until it is in his own authorial interest to divulge more. I mistakenly thought for about two thirds of the book that Pedro represented the reappearance of a central character in Wiesel's earlier novel, *The Town Beyond the Wall*. Both are named Pedro, both are redemptive presences, both comment astutely on the human scene, both give good advice and example to younger compatriots, both take inordinate risks to save others. But the earlier Pedro was explicitly not Jewish, while the Pedro of *Twilight* was originally named Pinhas, a fact that, just to make matters more ambiguous, is omitted from the English translation. (The creation of such dilemmas for the reader is vintage Wiesel.)

But whoever Pedro may be, he not only tracks Raphael down after the war as a Jewish child with no family left and therefore in need of help, but subsequently promises to rescue Raphael's brother, Yoel, when it is discovered that Yoel is in a psychiatric ward in Krasnograd. Pedro makes elaborate plans for the rescue and estimates the odds of succeeding on this wild mission at fifty-fifty.

The odds are insufficient. The attempt fails. Yoel does not escape. Pedro does not return.

Much of Raphael Lipkin's subsequent life is devoted to finding out what happened to Pedro, and to securing his freedom if he is still alive. Several years later, after writing a laudatory article about Pedro, Raphael begins to receive ugly, anonymous phone calls that impugn Pedro's integrity, asserting that after his capture he became an informer. The calls leave Raphael outraged and frustrated, until the caller cryptically suggests that he go to the Mountain Clinic where he may perhaps receive enlightenment about the "true" Pedro.

So Rafael goes to the Mountain Clinic. He starts interviewing patients, ostensibly to continue scholarly research on mysticism and madness. We wait with mounting suspense for a denouement in which the mystery of Pedro will be unveiled and the calumnies against him exposed for what they are. Is he one of the biblically inspired madmen? Has one of the members of the staff had contact with him elsewhere? Is someone at the clinic the originator of the mysterious phone calls, perhaps the equally mysterious Dr. Benedictus himself?

How neatly the threads of these three stories could have been woven together by a second-rate novelist. But how true to his theme and the lives of his characters Wiesel is by refusing to succumb to such an artifice. And how powerfully communicative of the uncertainty that persists for all Holocaust "survivors," that the threads of the many stories do *not* come together, and that ambiguity has the last word. Raphael even wonders at one point whether the phone calls were simply the product of his demented imagination.

The title is, after all, *Twilight,* a time when things are ambiguous, hard to see, and our vision plays tricks on us. Wiesel's first three books are entitled *Night, Dawn,* and *Day* (the latter rendered as *The Accident* in English). *Night* was the story of his time in Auschwitz and its title was grimly and straightforwardly descriptive. Both *Dawn* and *Day,* however, were ironic titles, describing what turned out to be the moral cul-de-sacs of being an executioner, or engaging in flight to exorcize the searing experience of "the kingdom of night." *Twilight,* like *Night,* seems to be a descriptive rather than an ironic title. "Twilight," as Raphael informs Pedro, "is the domain of madness" (p. 202). It is the time when things often appear other than they are, and vision is not as keen as one would wish. It is the time of madmen, for whom ambiguity is the only clarity they know, who may see clearly in the twilight hour things that are hidden from the rest of us.

Friendship and God

It is in the twilight, therefore, that the climactic interview with "God" takes place. Raphael's bags are packed, a farewell dinner has been held, and yet before going to the station he takes a final walk around the grounds of the asylum, sensing intuitively that there is something more he has to learn before his departure.

And there he finds, as though waiting for him, the patient who thinks he is God. God is brooding over the way creation has gone astray. Raphael feels a need to pursue the subject. Where, after all, is the divine pity, and why has it always been used so sparingly? How can God justify all the human suffering, of which Raphael has seen more than his share?

While taken aback by Raphael's insistent probing, God attempts a response. God "could have prevented the killer from being born, his accomplice from growing up, mankind from going astray. . . ." Yes. But there is still a problem: "Can you tell me," God asks Raphael, "at what precise moment I should have intervened to keep the children from being thrown into the flames? At the very last moment? Why not before? But when is 'before'?" (p. 208). God turns the enigma back to the interlocutor.

Raphael responds, first calmly and then in agitation, "Merciful God, God of Love, where were you and where was your love when under the seal of blood and fire the killers obliterated thousands of Jewish communities?" (p. 209). These are words, Raphael tells himself, "demanding to be spoken."

God, described now by Wiesel as "the patient," is deeply hurt. And Raphael, discerning what he thinks are tears on the cheeks of the other, regrets his harsh words.

But after an interlude in which Raphael remembers three individual heartrending episodes that illustrate God's complicity with human evil (of the sort we encountered in our study of *Ani Maamin*), the conversation continues. God urges Raphael not to cry for himself. Rather, "Cry for the others. And for me too" (p. 213). The last four words seem to have been wrenched out of God's mouth. Are we to cry not only *to* God but *for* God? Could God need human beings to share God's burden of sorrow, as much as human beings need God to share their burden of sorrow? The theme echoes an exegesis of Ecclesiastes that a Midrashic scholar had once shared with Raphael: *we must pity God*.

The mystery of evil is not resolved in this interview with the patient who thinks he is God. It will never be solved in any interview, no matter who the participants are. But the exchange provides the possibility of a new link between ourselves and God. Yes, we must challenge God, we must question God, we must be angry with God, we must even on occasion rebuke God. But we can also, in the words of the Midrashic master, "pity God." God, too, is saddened by the state of creation. God, too, feels the pain of others. We can believe that it is a pain that wounds the heart of God as well as the hearts of God's children. Perhaps such recognition is a way of coming closer to God.

Further credence is given to this suggestion when we reflect on the name of the novel's protagonist, chosen (as in all Wiesel's novels) with special care. In *Twilight,* the name of the protagonist is Rapha-el, which means "the healer of God," or as it can also be rendered, "God the Healer," leaving us with a creative ambiguity. Perhaps in heaven as on earth it is true that the only authentic healer is a wounded healer.

God and Friendship

But the novel does not end in heaven. It ends on earth. What remains, at the end, when the author refuses to let the plot fall into a tidy pattern on either the human or the divine level? What remains is something positive in the midst of much that is negative—a celebration of human friendship. In a world that seemed continually to scoff at the notion that anything like friendship or commitment or concern could survive, it was an act of courage to be committed to anything, let alone anybody. We are privileged to share in the creation of deep bonds between two brave people—Pedro and Raphael—people who will risk everything for the sake of the others, people who enlist our admiration because at a time when it would have been easy for either of them to turn inward and say, "I've suffered enough," both were willing to turn outward and say, "There are people who have suffered too much; we must help them."

Is this enough to "justify" a creation that scars all survivors and destroys all victims? Raphael and God are still debating that question at the end of the novel, and their counterparts will be doing so until the end of time. But, as Wiesel says again and again, it is the questions, not the answers, that are important. We will never know the answers, but we can keep refining the questions and refusing to surrender them to easy speculation, relentlessly pursuing what can never be found but must always be sought.

One cannot chart the future of a creative artist. Perhaps not even an artist like Wiesel knows what will come next, and if he does he must always be open to events that may intervene powerfully enough to cause a change of direction. Even so, I am intrigued by the possibilities of a continuation in the sequence that goes, so far, *Night, Dawn, Day, Twilight*. What comes next? A demon, perhaps, suggests a volume entitled *Midnight,* exploring the profound Kierkegaardian question in *Either/Or,* "Do you not know that there comes a midnight hour when all must unmask?"

What Wiesel could do with such a theme. . . .

6

THE AFFIRMATION AND NEGATION OF IMAGES
Charles Williams

Of all the novelists considered in this book, the name of Charles Williams is probably the least familiar. This initially presented itself as a reason to exclude him, had it not suddenly occurred to me that it was a capital reason to make sure he was included, since he represents a point of view that, while not widespread, contributes to our understanding of the world we live in and the way a novelist can deepen that understanding. Since Williams wrote in many genres, we cannot do justice to him without occasional consideration of other writing besides his works of fiction.

Who was Charles Williams? The outer events of his life were relatively unexciting, just as the outer events in his finest novel, *Descent Into Hell,* were relatively unexciting: a group of amateurs got together and produced a play. Williams was employed by the Oxford University Press, worked behind a desk in London, and had what C. S. Lewis called "a brilliantly happy marriage." When the war came, his office was evacuated to Oxford, and he lived there until his unexpected death in 1945. While at Oxford, he became acquainted with a group of dons, self-styled "The Inklings," who used to meet in Lewis's rooms at Magdalen College on Thursday evenings, and on Tuesday mornings in "the best of all public-houses for draught cider, whose name it would be madness to reveal."[1] These sessions were highlighted not only by draught cider and discussion, but also by a sharing of the manuscripts on which the members were working. All of Williams's last novel, *All Hallows' Eve,* was subjected to the criticism of this group.

Williams also lectured at the university during the war years, chiefly in

English literature. His teaching increasingly attracted the attention of the undergraduates, who, on the occasion of some lectures on Milton, "filled the benches listening first with incredulity, then with toleration, and finally with delight, to something so strange and new in their experience as the praise of chastity."[2]

There was no situation in which his closest friends would have felt him to be at a loss. T. S. Eliot writes:

> I have always believed that he would have been equally at ease in every kind of supernatural company; that he would never have been surprised or disconcerted by the intrusion of any visitor from another world, whether kindly or malevolent; and that he would have shown exactly the same natural ease and courtesy, with an exact awareness of how one should behave, to an angel, a demon, a human ghost, or an elemental. For him there was no frontier between the material and the spiritual world. Had I ever had to spend a night in a haunted house, I should have felt secure with Williams in my company.[3]

Here is an area where Williams the man and Williams the writer are one, for the novels are full of commerce between two worlds (only Williams would never have called them "two worlds") which at first strikes a reader as weird and strange, but which to any friend of Williams would seem only in character. In his novels he shares a dimension of experience denied to most of us but known intimately to himself.

This side of Williams's personality was confirmed by his death. His Oxford friends have reported their experience of "the ubiquitous presence of a dead man, as if he had ceased to meet us in particular places in order to meet us everywhere," and C. S. Lewis has written, "No event has so corroborated my faith in the next world as Williams did simply by dying. When the idea of death and the idea of Williams thus met in my mind, it was the idea of death that was changed."[4]

If, as T. S. Eliot says, the man and his writings were the same, an impression of Williams can be sharpened by a recital of the kinds of writing he did.

He was a literary critic, and his work on Dante (*The Figure of Beatrice*), Milton (Preface to *The Poetical Works of Milton*), and various volumes on poetry (*Poetry at Present, The English Poetic Mind*, etc.) are outstanding in their field. He was a playwright, who wrote for many specific occasions, including the Canterbury Festival. He was a poet, as C. S. Lewis thought, a major poet, whose poetry may become one of the most significant literary contributions of the twentieth century.

He was a "lay theologian" as well, and some of his most suggestive ideas are found in his frankly theological works, such as *The Descent of the Dove*, a history of the Holy Spirit in the life of the church; *He Came Down from Heaven,* an account of the biblical drama of creation, the fall, and redemption; and *The Forgiveness of Sins,* an acute dealing with one of the most difficult problems of Christian theology.

Also, and most important for our purposes, Williams was a novelist, one of those novelists whose works not only have a surface appeal, in that they are entertaining stories, but which also have layers of meaning that are gradually penetrated with each rereading. Of the seven novels, *Descent Into Hell* and *All Hallows' Eve* are of preeminent worth and importance as conveyers of some of Williams's most central ideas, but there is not one of them that does not contain flashes of penetrating insight. The novels are sometimes referred to in Britain as "spiritual shockers," or murder mysteries set in eternity, a kind of high-class science fiction without much science. Williams writes in a manner that can only be described as "fascinating," in the best sense of that much-abused word. He is quite literally able to hold readers spellbound, to captivate them. As the writer of this chapter knows, it is dangerous to read him in a subway; he carries the reader past the intended destination. Not many people will put down *War in Heaven* once they have read the first sentence of the first chapter: "The telephone bell was ringing wildly, but without result, since there was no-one in the room but the corpse."

Williams's theological perspective is Anglo-Catholic, and he treasures the tradition as one that is rich and fertile. What might be called his "catholic orthodoxy," is, however, not the pedestrian, acquiescent kind that manages to survive in the modern world by the simple expedient of refusing to ask questions. On the contrary, he felt it was not only possible but mandatory for us to question God. (Here is one of the few matters on which Williams and Elie Wiesel might agree.) Williams had little patience with the pious person who says, "Our little minds were never meant to question God." Williams replies, "Fortunately there is the book of Job to make it clear that our little minds were meant. A great curiosity ought to exist concerning divine things. Man was intended to argue with God."[5] As Lewis put it:

> [Williams] did not believe that God himself wanted that frightened, indignant, and voluble creature to be annihilated; or even silenced. If it wanted to carry its hot complaints to the very Throne, even that, he felt, would be a permitted absurdity. For was not that very much what Job had done? It was true, Williams added, that the Divine answer had taken the surprising form of inviting Job to study the hippopotamus and the crocodile. But Job's impatience had been approved. His apparent blasphemies had been accepted. The weight of the divine displeasure had been reserved for the "comforters," the self-appointed advocates on God's side, the people who tried to show that all was well.[6]

Four Themes

Certain themes constantly reappear in Williams's writings.

1. A fundamental motif may be called *the interpenetration of the two worlds,* although we have already discovered that Williams would have been unhappy with the phrase. He did not believe in a two-story (let alone a medieval three-story) universe. The suggestion that there is a "material" realm and a "spiritual" realm would have shocked him. The phrase may stand, however, in order that we may understand how Williams knocks down a barrier (between "two worlds") that does not really exist and is simply of human devising. Since the terminology seems unavoidable, T. S. Eliot's comment may stand: "To him the supernatural was perfectly natural, and the natural was also supernatural." Williams has succeeded in introducing the dimension of the supernatural into human life and making it seem not only credible, but incredibly enough, natural.

No sharp lines can be drawn between heaven and earth, and, much more surprisingly and much more profoundly, none can be drawn between past, present, and future. This aspect of Williams's thought, baffling to the uninitiated, must be grasped if his novels are to be appreciated. In them, people living three hundred years apart help each other bear suffering; the keeper of the Holy Grail talks with the rector of a village church; a stone transports people through time and space; a magician conjures up the likenesses of other people by incantation; a deck of cards starts a seemingly endless snowstorm; a girl wanders through London even though she is dead (and we don't realize she is dead for a long time). The point is that the whole cosmos is all of a piece. It is one and it is God's—through all time and space, beyond all time and space.

2. That idea grasped, it is possible to understand more fully what is probably the most important single ethical concept for Williams, *the practice of substituted love.* It is his way of responding to the Pauline formula, "Bear ye one another's burdens." It means, to be very pedestrian, that we must continually help each other.

C. S. Lewis identified a hierarchy of levels in this total experience that may be briefly examined.[7] There is, first of all, *exchange;* in all our experience we recognize that we live by the services of others. Elayne and her women (in Williams' Arthurian poems) bake what the men have sown and harvested, and thus exchange takes place. Williams often uses the simple example of loaning a book to a friend. In *Descent Into Hell* he points out that the women in the Scilly

Islands wash *each others'* laundry, thus giving the deed further meaning. (As I write this, my four-year-old son and his best friend have just "exchanged" their bedroom slippers, and are in an infectious transport of ecstacy.)

Substitution involves a higher degree of giving and receiving. Individuals voluntarily consent to bear the fear or the burden that properly belongs to someone else: If your resources are inadequate for the occasion, I will lend you mine. Williams illustrates it from the history of the church. Felicitas, going to her death, is sustained because she believes, "Another will be in me who will suffer for me, as I shall suffer for him." Saint Anthony says, "Your life and death are in your neighbor." Christ puts it, "They in me and I in them."[8] This is the pattern of life, the web of glory.

Co-inherence involves seeing this process at work not only in oneself but in the whole universe as well, particularly in the act of substituted love which the death of Christ made manifest, and in the divine relationship of the persons of the Trinity.

The practice of substituted love can be illustrated from the novel *Descent Into Hell,* where it is most clearly described. Pauline Anstruther is constantly in terror because she sees her own image approaching her on the street. She is quite literally a "split personality." Peter Stanhope makes the apparently ridiculous suggestion that she let him carry her fear for her, "like a parcel." Overcoming her astonishment, she does so, and to her even greater astonishment finds that she is no longer afraid. Since he carries the fear, she is released from it.

This is the beginning of her salvation, and with precise psychological perception, Williams puts her temptation at this point, the temptation to have "peace of mind" by shutting "everything but yourself out." She can resist this partly because she is wanted; her salvation must be completed. It is not enough for her to get rid of her burden, she must accept another's burden. She offers to carry the burden of her dying grandmother, but the burden that will be hers to carry opens up "a world of such incredible dimensions" that she is breathless at the thought. She is to bear the fear of her dead ancestor who had died a martyr's death three hundred years before. In a vision she sees him, fearing the fire, and in an impulse of love she takes that burden of fear upon herself: "Give it to me, John Struther," says her own voice, behind her. It is her other self, the one she had been afraid to meet, and in the act of substituted love her wholeness is restored, while Struther, going to the stake, can cry out in triumph, "I have seen the salvation of my God."

This is life: a great web of exchange, of people bearing one another's burdens. Peter Stanhope must bear Pauline's. Pauline must bear John

Struther's. Of Christ himself it was said, "he saved others; himself he cannot save." We cannot save ourselves; we must save others.

The practice of substituted love is not merely a theoretical possibility for Williams. He seriously believed that we could and should carry one another's burdens, and that there was a technique for doing it. All life is to be vicarious. The technique, he says, needs practice and intelligence. Above all,

> The one who gives has to remember that he has parted with his burden, that it is being carried by another, that his part is to believe that and be at peace. . . . The one who takes has to set himself—mind, emotion and sensation—to the burden, to know it, imagine it, receive it—and sometimes not be taken aback by the swiftness of the divine grace and the lightness of the burden.[9]

3. For our purposes, Williams's most important contribution is his treatment of *The Ways of the Affirmation and Negation of Images.* The matter at stake is how persons are to view themselves and the created world in their ultimate relation to God. To what degree do the images of our earthly life give us clues about the nature of ultimate reality? Williams sees that there have been two main approaches to this problem. There is first what can be called the romantic way, *the affirmation of images.* There are "images," experiences, events of human life, that can testify to us of God. Every created thing, according to this view, partially reveals God, and can help us back to God. Williams finds the principle expressed in the phrase of Athanasius, "Not by the conversion of the Godhead into flesh, but by taking of the manhood into God."

The greatest exponent of the way of affirmation did not emerge until Dante, since the church had first to stress, says Williams, "the awful difference between God and the world before we would be permitted to see the awful likeness."[10] Dante saw the "awful likeness." It was in the "Beatrician experience," as he gazed at his beloved, that Dante saw for a moment a human being as God sees and intends that human being to be. Williams colloquially translates the passage of the *Vita Nuova* after Dante has seen Beatrice, as follows:

> I say that when she came along I was so thrilled with the mere hope that she would notice me that I was friends with everyone, and utterly full of goodwill, and I was ready to forgive anyone who had offended me. If I had been asked any question at all I should have answered quite humbly *Love.*[11]

The comment by Williams is that the sight of Beatrice "filled him with the fire of charity and clothed him with humility: he became—and for a moment he knew it—an entire goodwill."[12] As Dante affirms the image of Beatrice, he can say to God of her, as can all other upholders of the way of affirmation, "This also is Thou . . ."

It is because Williams believed in the way of the affirmation of images that he dwelt at such length on what he called *the theology of romantic love.* This meant not that one is romantic about theology but that one is theological about romance. Romantic love can be a kind of stepping stone leading toward the love of God. The poets understand this. Dante experienced it. Milton sensed it also; for him, "Eve is at once an inhabitant of the kingdom and the means by which the kingdom is seen."[13] Thus the experience of "falling in love" can have affinities with the experience of coming to love God. What Williams does, in other words, is to use "the universal experience of falling in love as a starting point for enabling us to see something of the meaning of the claim of theology to be the divine wisdom which opens our eyes to the meaning of all things."[14]

Thus the way of the affirmation of images. But there has been another way as well, the ascetic way, or *the rejection of images,* the rejection, that is, of all images save God. If advocates of the first position can say, "This also is Thou," advocates of the second continually remind themselves, "Neither is this Thou." No created thing is more than an image, an image that can become an idol. So the images must be rejected. There are abundant instances of this pattern as well in Christian thought. The early Christian ascetics rejected the world and the "images" of God it contained. Most of the mystics have done likewise; Williams's favorite example is Dionysius the Aereopagite who can only say what God is *not.* The author of *The Cloud of Unknowing* follows the way of negation, as do Saint John of the Cross and (for Williams at any rate) Kierkegaard. This has been the more usual path of recorded sanctity.

However—and this is the point of Williams's discussion of the two ways—*both ways must be followed by everyone.* If the way of affirmation by itself leads to idolatry, the way of negation by itself leads to gnosticism and the rejection of God's creation. So the two ways must coexist. Rejection can be rejection but it cannot be denial; reception can be reception but it cannot be subservience.[15]

> Neither of these two Ways indeed is, or can be, exclusive. The most vigorous ascetic, being forbidden formally to hasten his death, is bound to attend to the actualities of food, drink, and sleep which are also images, however brief his attention may be. The most indulgent Christian is yet bound to hold his most cherished images—of food, drink, sleep, or anything else—negligible beside the final Image of God.[16]

So of all images, the Christian must always say, "This also is Thou; neither is this Thou." Williams uses the phrase continually, and it sums up his understanding of the two Ways.[17] Throughout the range of his writings Williams uses device after device to insist upon the dual emphasis. In *War in*

Heaven, an early novel, Williams has the Archdeacon greet the Holy Grail, one of the supreme images of Christendom, with the words, "Neither is this Thou," after which, but only after which, he says, "Yet this also is Thou."[18] In the poem "The Departure of Dindrane," in *The Region of the Summer Stars,* he shows how those who follow one of the two ways must also accept the other. Dindrane, on her way to the convent (the way of rejection) says, "I will affirm, my beloved, all that I should." Taliessin, on his way to Camelot (the way of affirmation) says, "I will reject all that I should." Williams suggests that even in one so committed to the way of rejection as Saint John of the Cross, the element of affirmation is not totally lacking:

> Even he, toward the end, was encouraged to remember that he liked asparagus: our Lord the Spirit is reluctant to allow either of the two great Ways to flourish without some courtesy to the other.[19]

4. A final image in Williams's writing is *the City.* The image is taken from the City in the New Testament book of Revelation. The City, there and elsewhere, is the pattern of the new creation. Pauline, in *Descent Into Hell,* once she has achieved, through the act of substituted love for her dead ancestor, her citizenship in the City, realizes that she is in heaven, though she hardly dares say it. In *All Hallows' Eve,* when Lester Furnival enters the City after she has redeemed her dead past into love, she comes to see that in the City "citizenship meant relationship and knew it; its citizens lived new acts or lived the old at will. What on earth is only in the happiest moments of friendship or love was now normal."[20]

As is so frequent in Williams, the heavenly image is often close to an earthly one. In such novels as *Descent Into Hell* and *All Hallows' Eve* one is not always quite sure whether "the City" is the heavenly one or London itself. The images cannot be completely separated. London, to Williams, was an image to be affirmed. To him it represented something akin to *order,* one of the basic elements in the City. Order, that is, as opposed to chaos and disorder. ("Hell is inaccurate," Williams once wrote.) The City is the manifestation of the divine order, in which human beings, through grace and the "divine condescension," can participate. One of Williams's most pleasant analogies occurs in *War in Heaven,* where he describes a run-down old residential street. However, new life is starting at one end of the street, for there "a public house signalized the gathering of another code of decency and morals which might in time transform the intervening decay."[21] (American readers need to realize that a public house—a "pub"—is a place where people gather to drink together, a place which is, however, unlike an American bar.) There is in a public house, as C. S. Lewis points out, a "proletarian courtesy and community . . . with all the mutual forbearance and observance of unwritten law which . . . are a manifestation of 'the city.' "[22] In this experience of orderliness and courtesy Williams could see an image of the city of God.

In more conventional theological terms, Williams identified the City as the apocalyptic understanding of the kingdom of God, "the state into which Christendom is called; but, except in vision, she is not yet the City. The City is the state which the Church is to become."[23] The City thus "descends to Patmos and the world," in "its web of exchanged glory."[24] Even we can see flashes and hints of the City of which Christ is "the President" (*The Figure of Beatrice*) or the "Lord Mayor" (*All Hallows' Eve*). Williams, however, saw more than most of us, and in an affirmation of co-inherence, has shared his vision with us.

These and other aspects of Williams's thought may sound initially strange, especially to American Protestant Christians. And yet there are few writers who can help us to overcome some of our excessively American Protestant biases more convincingly than Williams, or who can better help us see the "wholeness" of the faith, much of which we have cavalierly discarded. Those who turn to him, if they approach his writings with what Williams would call the "courtesy" of an open mind, will discover in him a means of grace, through whom the mystery of life becomes more sacred, the mysteries of the kingdom (or the City) more luminous, and the central mystery of Christendom more blessed.

III

7

GRACE IN THE MIDST OF JUDGMENT?
Albert Camus, *The Fall*

Albert Camus was clearly and explicitly not a Christian, nor even a theist, but he was unwilling to accept an alternative that approached nihilism or even an existentialism of the Jean Paul Sartre variety. His early book of essays, *The Myth of Sisyphus,* came to the conclusion that even in a meaningless universe, suicide is not permitted. His novel *The Plague* was a sensitive portrayal of people fulfilling the call of duty and even love, in a situation where duty and love were vulnerable and liable to extinction. To him, the world remained absurd (*ab-surdus,* very deaf), not even hearing, much less responding to, humanity's plaintive cry for meaning.

And yet, although Camus vigorously rejected the Christian option, he continued to do battle with it, and the swordplay was rather vigorous for one who considered that his enemy was long since dead. We have no right to turn Camus into a kind of crypto-Christian, but we can at least see that he was dealing with many themes that concern Christians, and that the way in which he deals with those themes should be of concern to Christians.

His novel *The Fall* gives us the self-portrait of a "contemporary," who is making a kind of secular confession, in which the reader plays the part of the listener. We hear the story of a man's "fall"; yet as we discover toward the end, this is not just the fall of a particular human being, but the fall of humanity as a whole. The narrator is not just telling his own story, but in a real and disturbing sense is telling us our own story.

Why John the Baptist?

We make the acquaintance of the speaker in a small bar in Amsterdam. Since he is obviously a man of culture, we immediately wonder how he ended up in such a dive. He introduces himself as Jean-Baptiste Clamence. And here we must linger, for the book is too full of biblical allusions for us to believe that the name is chosen by Camus without deliberate intent. Why is the narrator called John the Baptist?

There are a number of ways to answer this question. John the Baptist came preaching judgment. With remarkable success he convicted his hearers of sin and made them aware of the evils of their generation. Jean-Baptiste displays considerable skill in achieving similar ends.

A second conjecture would be that the biblical figure of John the Baptist is chosen by Camus as a forerunner of salvation, pointing the way toward someone yet to come through whom a resolution of the human dilemma might be effected. But although this may be the most authentic meaning of the biblical figure, it is hardly descriptive of the Camus figure, for there are no more than slight and elusive hints of any kind of salvation in his message.

It would seem more likely, therefore, that there is a monumental irony in Camus giving the last word in this book to Jean-Baptiste. It is as though he were saying to us, in effect, "This may be a world sadly in need of redemption, but we have no grounds for hoping either that it has been redeemed or that it will be redeemed. It is a world into which a John the Baptist can come, but not a world into which a messiah can come."

Camus's choice of a last name for his protagonist—Clamence—only heightens the ambiguity and the irony, for the prophet of the Exile, cited in Isaiah 40, who offers a hope not yet realized, is described in the Vulgate (the Latin translation of the Hebrew scriptures) as a "voice crying in the wilderness," *Vox clamantis in deserto*, whose message is "Prepare the way for the Lord!" If there is ever to be cause for rejoicing, it is going to be considerably deferred.

Withal, there remains a very biblical thrust to Jean-Baptiste. Early in the monologue he says to his as yet unsuspecting listener, "Do you have any possessions? Some? Good. Have you shared them with the poor? No? Then you are what I call a Sadducee. If you are not familiar with the Scriptures, I admit that this won't help you" (p. 9. Luke 3:11 and Matt. 3:7–8 may be of assistance to readers in this latter category). So the impact of the first exchange is: we have possessions, yes. We have not shared them with the poor, no. We are Sadducees. Jean-Baptiste is already beginning to make us uncomfortable.

We gradually learn more about him and discover why he needs to probe beneath his own vanity. He had been a lawyer in Paris who specialized in what he called "noble" causes; that is to say, he defended "widows and orphans, as the saying goes" (p. 17). "As the saying goes," indeed. The saying goes: "Religion that is pure and undefiled before God and the Father is this: to visit orphans and widows in their affliction, and to keep oneself unstained from the world" (James 1:27). And while Jean-Baptiste may not have taken the latter part of this definition seriously, he was assuredly trying to do good works. His whole aim in life was to help people. He liked to give alms, to assist the blind across the street, to win a case and charge no fee. (He tells us, rather arrogantly, how he was never arrogant about these things.) He was very popular. He was a social success. He was, before his time, a positive thinker. This was the period of life which he describes as being "in Eden," life before "the fall."

The Devastation of Self-Awareness

But one evening, he heard a laugh behind him. He turned around and no one was there. It seemed to him to be the laughter of judgment.

And now self-awareness begins to dawn in the life of Jean-Baptiste. He sees that what he really wants to do is not help but dominate other lives. He sees, worse yet, that he is a hypocrite, a play actor:

> Why, shortly after the evening I told you about [i.e., the scream of laughter which began to dislodge his totally secure universe], I discovered something. When I would leave a blind man on the sidewalk to which I had conveyed him, I used to tip my hat to him. Obviously the hat tipping wasn't intended for him, since he couldn't see it. To whom was it addressed? To the public. After playing my part, I would take the bow." (p. 47)

And so it pours out. What is revealed in this apparently trivial incident is basic to what Jean-Baptiste really is. "I was always bursting with vanity. I, I, I, is the refrain of my whole life, which could be heard in everything I said" (p. 48).

This kind of analysis begins to strike home to the reader. Are we not also described by this candid self-revelation? What are our motives for doing good? Do we do our alms to be seen by others? Could we ever settle for entering into our closets to pray, as Jesus proposes? The New Testament is hovering in the background all the time, much to our discomfort.

Jean-Baptiste discovers the same thing to be true about his relations with women, and he fancied himself, not without some justification, a great lover. He saw that he didn't really mean what he said to women. He was a spectator to his own affairs, watching them without emotion or involvement. And more devastatingly, he came to see that this was true of his intercessions for the widows and orphans. He was putting on a show there too. The whole thing was not centered on them, but on himself.

> On my own admission, I could live happily only on condition that all the
> individuals on earth, or the greatest possible number, were turned toward me,
> eternally in suspense, devoid of independent life and ready to answer my call at any
> moment, doomed in short to sterility until the day I should deign to favor them. In
> short, for me to live happily it was essential for the creatures I chose not to live at
> all. They must receive their life, sporadically, only at my bidding. (p. 68)

One would have to look far and wide in the annals of Christian theology to
find a more chillingly accurate description of original sin. Augustine could
have written *nihil obstat* under such words.

Jean-Baptiste has been preparing us for a description of the defining event
of his downward pilgrimage. It seems disappointing at first in its simplicity.
Two or three years before he heard the laughter, something happened, the
import of which finally caught up with him. He was walking home over the
Seine and saw a woman leaning over the railing of the bridge. He walked on,
heard the sound of a body striking the water, heard a cry repeated several
times, heard an interminable silence. He wanted to run but he didn't stir. He
knew he should be quick but he did nothing. Slowly he walked away. He
informed no one. And for the next few days, as he informs us, he didn't read
the papers.

Judgment Cannot Be Dodged

Now what happens to Jean-Baptiste after this event? More and more his
self-sufficient world caves in. His facade of helpfulness, nobility, and charity
collapses. He feels himself under judgment:

> *Mon cher ami*, let's not give them any pretext, no matter how small, for judging
> us! Otherwise, we'll be left in shreds. . . . I realized this all at once the moment I
> had the suspicion that maybe I wasn't so admirable. From then on, I became
> distrustful. (p. 77)

Even his friends now seem to him to be laughing at him. They, too, have an
irresistible vocation for judgment. But it is the other laugh that continues to
gnaw away at the innards of Jean-Baptiste, and he realizes that there is
laughter, there is judgment, even when there is no one to be observed
laughing or judging. From this there is no escape, as Jean-Baptiste finally
realizes when he says, "The whole universe then began to laugh at me" (p. 80).

And this is what he tries, unsuccessfully, to dodge. Not being able to dodge
it, Jean-Baptiste realizes that he must confess his lies about himself—confess
to someone (not to God, since "God is out of style") before he dies and death
makes the lies definitive.

This was a decision of desperation, reached only after he had sought to escape judgment by debauchery and discovered that this cul-de-sac led only to the "little-ease." The "little-ease" was an ingenious medieval torture chamber. It was nothing but a prison cell too small to stand in upright, and too narrow to lie down in at full length. People were left there for years, learning more and more that they were guilty and that "innocence consists in stretching joyously" (p. 110). Jean-Baptiste could not stretch joyously. But neither, he decided, could anyone else: "we cannot assert the innocence of anyone, whereas we can state with certainty the guilt of all. Every man testifies to the crime of all the others—that is my faith and my hope" (p. 110).

His own awareness of his predicament is heightened by an attempt to shrug off his guilt through debauchery. Thinking he is finally cured, he goes on a sea voyage, but off in the distance he sees a speck and thinks it is a drowning person; the cry ringing over the Seine many years ago is still ringing in his ears. He cannot escape it. He will hear it everywhere, "everywhere, in short, where lies the bitter water of my baptism." He continues this figure of speech by crying out that he can never escape from "this immense holy-water font." Here is a John the Baptist who has himself not been baptized; he may have descended into the tomb (one of the early images in the moment of submersion beneath the water), but he has not risen from it to the promised "newness of life."

He is not too worried about a last judgment, because he has known something worse, human judgment. "I'll tell you a big secret, *mon cher*. Don't wait for the Last Judgment. It takes place every day" (p. 111)—a perfect mirroring of the conclusion of Franz Kafka we have previously noted, that only our sense of time makes it possible to speak of a "last" judgment, since the court that issues such condemnations is in perpetual session. Such judgment, both for Jean-Baptiste and for Joseph K, is the most terrifying of all, for it acknowledges no extenuating circumstances. People now judge even in the name of Christ, though he himself spoke softly to the adulteress and said, "Neither do I condemn thee." But people, on their part, condemn without absolving.

The "Judge-Penitent"

Is this terrifying sense of daily and unremitting judgment to be the last word? Jean-Baptiste claims to have found a way out. There is only one way to silence that midnight cry of laughter and judgment: "It is essential to begin by extending the condemnation to all, without distinction, in order to thin it out at the start" (p. 131). There must be no excuses for anyone. There must be no acknowledgment of the good intention, the extenuating circumstance.

Everything must be totted up: "I am for any theory that refuses to grant man innocence and for any practice that treats him as guilty" (pp. 131–132).

To Jean-Baptiste, this means becoming what he calls a "judge-penitent." He closes his law office, moves to Amsterdam, and decides to indulge in public confession at every opportunity, not so much to secure his own innocence as to implicate his hearers in guilt. We discover that this is what he has been doing from page one. When he has finished painting a portrait of Jean-Baptiste, he not only says, "I show it with great sorrow: 'This, alas, is what I am!' The prosecutor's charge is finished" (p. 140). He also says, "But at the same time the portrait I hold out to my contemporaries becomes a mirror."

> I stand before all humanity recapitulating my shames without losing sight of the effect I am producing, and saying, "I was the lowest of the low." Then imperceptibly I pass from the "I" to the "we." When I get to "This is what we are," the trick has been played and I can tell them off. I am like them, to be sure; we are in the soup together. (p. 140)

The judgment has indeed been thinned out to include all. We have ourselves been brought into the circle of the guilty. Not only does Jean-Baptiste claim the right to judge us, but he provokes us into judging ourselves. We have known him less than a week, and we are not yet ready to accept his offer that we confess our sins to him. But he has upset us: "Admit, however," he proposes, "that today you feel less pleased with yourself than you felt five days ago?" (p. 141).

In the final pages, Jean-Baptiste suggests a little wistfully that his solution is not *quite* foolproof: "At long intervals, on a really beautiful night I occasionally hear a distant laugh and again I doubt. But quickly I crush everything, people and things, under the weight of my own infirmity, and at once I perk up" (p. 142). So there is still a tiny chink in his armor. He has not totally resolved his problem, although he thinks he has gotten it under control.

Hearing and Listening

Camus has said in a newspaper interview that the theme of the novel centers on the wish, "If only for one minute we could forget ourselves for someone else." Jean-Baptiste is not a man who needs to be made aware of sin, for he is very much aware of it. He also knows all about judgment, and he even knows something about what is necessary on his side in dealing with judgment, which is to confess. He acknowledges his need. He sees his solidarity in evil with all people, and all people's solidarity in evil with him.

These are clearly themes with which Christianity (and many other religions) constantly grapple. Jean-Baptiste is clearly one to whom the message of grace, absolution, and forgiveness could in principle speak. But since God is now "out of style," there is no more for it than that. And Jean-Baptiste is uncertain whether or not he is within hearing distance of a God who listens, for God (if there is a God) may be deaf.

But it is just possible that he may be closer to a state of grace than are many conventional Christians—those who think they listen all the time, but do not bring themselves within hearing distance. Jean-Baptiste is living in a world into which Christ has not come—to him. But if we believe that this is a world into which Christ *has* come, we need not totally despair of Jean-Baptiste. As long as he remains unsatisfied with himself as he is, as long as he still, occasionally, on beautiful nights, hears the laughter of judgment, however softly, it is possible that he may one time hear something else—the more penetrating laughter of joy, which says, "Neither do I condemn thee. Go and sin no more."

We must honor Camus's integrity by keeping a question mark within our chapter title and not claiming for him a redemption he did not experience or count on. But there are enough hints in his writing of a mind and heart always on the move, that we may hope that one day the question mark will elongate itself into an exclamation point.

8

FRAGMENTS IN THE MIDST OF BROKENNESS
Alan Paton, *Too Late the Phalarope*

"There is a lovely road that runs from Ixopo into the hills. These hills are grass-covered and rolling, and they are lovely beyond any singing of it."

Many generations of school children could identify these words as the opening lines of Alan Paton's *Cry, the Beloved Country,* the poignant novel published in 1948 by the then principal of Diepkloof, a boys' reformatory in Johannesburg, South Africa. They were words that not only catapulted their unknown author to international fame, but helped introduce the rest of the world to injustices that had been perpetrated for generations in South Africa.

Unlike many of the authors discussed in these pages, Paton explicitly identified himself as a Christian and worked hard at *being* a Christian—not an easy task in a country where the government affirmed an understanding of Christianity that was diametrically opposed to Paton's understanding of Christianity. For decades he opposed the policies of his government, both directly in an unending flow of speeches and essays, and indirectly in his fiction.

It needs also to be said that in Alan Paton's later years history seemed to pass him by. He differed, for example, with black leaders like Desmond Tutu and Allan Boesak on the need for international economic sanctions against South Africa—sanctions that clearly have helped move South Africa toward a more open society. Paton will be remembered best, however, for his most active years, when he was among the fearless ones, creating enough animosity in high places so that his passport was revoked and for a decade he was a virtual political prisoner within the bounds of the country with which he had an enduring lover's quarrel.

And yet, Alan Paton, who died in 1988 full of years and wisdom, would not want to be remembered as a social reformer who wrote novels to advance a certain political agenda. The line between artistic creation and political propaganda is fatally easy to traverse, and Paton insisted that a novel must stand on its own *as a story*. If it also affects the way people deal with such social issues as apartheid, that is a happy plus, but it is not a reason to write a novel. When Paton took up his novelist's pen, he was conscious that he must remain true to the rules of his trade and not simply create a moralistic tract. After the unexpected success of *Cry, the Beloved Country,* he commented, "The most pleasing thing of all to me is that the critics, without exception, while recognizing this to be a book with a purpose, did not feel that here was another reformer prostituting the novel for his own ends. They felt the book to be of some literary value."

He developed a modest but exacting agenda. The novel, he wrote,

> will illuminate the road, but it will not lead the way with a lamp. It will expose the crevasse, but not provide the bridge. It will lance the boil, but not purify the blood. It cannot be expected to do more than this; and if we ask it to do more, we are asking too much. (*Knocking at the Door,* p. 146)

Cry, the Beloved Country has literary grace and sheer beauty, as even the single quotation at the beginning of this chapter bears witness, and in reading it one is simultaneously elevated by the style and sobered by the content. This double reaction is even truer of the second novel, *Too Late the Phalarope,* for while its predecessor was a story (as Paton called it) "of comfort in desolation," *Too Late the Phalarope* is, by contrast, a story full of "desolation" and singularly lacking in "comfort," unfolding the gradual but increasingly inevitable downfall of a good man. Set against the background of South African laws and customs, it is on one level a regional story, but on another and more important level it is a universal story—a story of how any person anywhere can be destroyed, not only by individual conceits and shortcomings but by brutal laws and loveless religion as well. How such a work can "persuade us to rejoice" is a matter we must face at the conclusion of the chapter; for the moment, the point to register is that Paton's sense of artistic integrity is so high that he will not permit religion to manipulate the plot in order to guarantee a "happy ending."

We have already made the acquaintance of various "Assyrians in modern dress," whose gift is to show us "a world without grace" so compelling that we are not tempted to settle for too-easy resolutions of deep conflicts. In Paton's case there is the added gift that while he, too, could describe clearly the reality of "a world without grace" and do so with great sensitivity, he could also describe the possibility of a world infused by grace, and provide instances throughout his book of the possibility of its transforming power. But in none of the instances does grace break through in a compelling enough way to redeem the situation, and in the end all the characters to whom we have been attracted (as well as those by whom we are repelled) are destroyed.

The German theologian Dietrich Bonhoeffer, in his struggle against the Nazi state, wrote about "cheap grace" that comes too easily, in contrast to "costly grace" that may mean bearing a cross. And it is a measure of the integrity of both Bonhoeffer and Paton that they refused to use religious palliatives to assuage their own social and individual conflicts. In both cases, in fact, the pervasive presence of the Christian church was part of the problem rather than part of the solution—in Bonhoeffer's case as an otherworldly Lutheranism disengaged from the struggle against an evil state, and in Paton's case as a harsh Calvinism that gave its blessing to an evil state.

Paton's narrative skill is exemplified in his style as well as his substance. The story is poignantly told through the eyes of Tante Sophie, a woman who believes that love and mercy must infuse human relationships, and watches helplessly as occasions for love and mercy dwindle and eventually disappear. She describes the destruction of a good man, her nephew Pieter van Vlaanderen, a police lieutenant who is also a football hero and a devout Christian. But Pieter, for all his outward attractiveness and apparent stability, is deeply torn within, being subject to "black moods" (a term Paton would probably not use in the 1990s) that come when least expected and lead to angry outbursts against subordinates, coldness toward his wife, a protective shield between himself and his father, and an illicit (and illegal) sexual liaison with Stephanie, a black woman. It is the exposing of the latter fact that destroys Pieter and his family.

With great understanding and sensitivity, Paton takes us inside Pieter's mind and soul; we see him torn apart, consumed with guilt after his initial encounter with Stephanie, and filled with terror that the act has been observed by others who are simply biding their time before destroying him. He bargains with God, making extravagant promises and imagining all sorts of divine interventions that will wipe out the reality of what he has done and give him a chance to atone. Sometimes the terror subsides, as an event of apparently fearful import dissolves into an innocent misunderstanding, but always the terror returns until he is finally confronted with circumstantial evidence so overwhelming that he cannot deny what he has done.

From then on, the succession of events is remorseless, for Pieter has violated the Immorality Act, a piece of legislation that prohibits sexual relations between the races—a law from which there are no extenuating circumstances, no mitigation of sentences, no possibility of forgiveness—nothing but destruction.

Contributors to the Downfall

What brings about the downfall of such a man, a character we cannot help but admire, a well-loved, well-known member of his community, who to all intents and purposes had a happy, creative, and fulfilled life?

Any answer to such a question is bound to be complex, so interwoven are human lives and destinies, and at one point Tante Sophie, looking for people to hold responsible, compiles a list that finally includes almost everyone in the story. Among them are several leading candidates.

The major contributor to his downfall must be *Pieter* himself. As we learn from his personal journal, he had a high degree of self-understanding about the two sides of his complex personality. He was capable of acts of personal generosity—quietly loaning money to a subordinate, Vorster, who is in deep financial distress, and even doing the same for the black girl Stephanie, who needs help to get through a difficult time with her child.

But when others were outgoing to Pieter, he tended to withdraw into an inner shell. This was particularly true when Tante Sophie tried to probe the cause of the "black moods"; she was dismissed by Pieter with a curtness and edge of outrage that hurt her deeply. In the presence of his overbearing father, Pieter endured parental rebuffs in silence. But when the "black moods" were upon him, Pieter could rip his subordinates apart. Much as he needed help—and knew that he needed help—he could not humble himself enough to open his inner being to another person.

In Pieter's eyes, *Nella,* his wife, was a major source of his difficulties. Sex with her husband was for Nella a thing more to be endured grimly than experienced joyously. Nella's religious upbringing in a strict family had conditioned her to believe that pleasure in sex was somehow wrong. Her religion made her less giving rather than more, and instilled in her a feeling that breaches of "modesty" were sinful. Her repeated retreats from fully sharing of herself only increased Pieter's sense that he was not truly affirmed where he needed affirmation most deeply. He wrote poignantly about this in his journal, and he attempted to persuade Nella that love was of the body as well as of the soul and that there was no distinction, but all belonged together:

> And I wanted to cry out at her that I could not put the body apart from the soul, and that the comfort of her body was more than a thing of the flesh, but was also a comfort of the soul, and why it was, I could not say, and why it should be, I

could not say, but there was in it nothing that was ugly or evil, but only good. But how can one find such words? (p. 86)

After a time away from Pieter, visiting her family, Nella returned and was beautifully sharing and self-giving, so much so that Pieter was transported to at least the third heaven. But almost immediately she retreated again to what she considered safer territory. Her rigidity caused the "black mood" to come upon Pieter once again, and with deliberate intent he "broke the law" by seeking out Stephanie.

The clearest example of the negative effect of rigid legalistic and judgmental Calvinism was *Jacob van Vlaanderen,* Pieter's father. Jacob felt that his son was effeminate to enjoy stamp collecting more than games with other boys, and he consequently forbade Pieter to collect stamps. Years later, when Pieter was grown and the father discovered that his son was collecting stamps secretly, he sneered at this use of time. When Pieter gave his father a pipe for his birthday, the father never once smoked it, a simple action that spoke volumes to the entire family about the near-contempt in which he held his son.

Jacob van Vlaanderen's religion was a religion of The Book, and he had a characteristically Calvinist ability to find the most judgmental, harsh, and merciless passages in The Book when they suited his own purposes. His harsh attitudes toward Pieter before Pieter's arrest for breaking the Immorality Act were child's play compared to his response when the news was announced. There was not a hint of concern or love. The family Bible was immediately gotten down and the name "Pieter van Vlaanderen" was scratched out again and again, until no record of his son remained in the family tree. The front door of the house was permanently locked. No one in the family was to have any trace of a continuing relationship with Pieter, on pain of being expelled from the household for good. All pictures of him, all possessions of his, anything he had ever given to any of them, were to be immediately destroyed. There was to be no mercy. Nor did Jacob van Vlaanderen spare himself. He wrote letters resigning his memberships in all of his clubs and totally cut himself off from friends and associates in the outside world.

And Jacob van Vlaanderen could find biblical warrant for all that he did. He read Psalm 109 aloud to his family minutes after their disgrace was revealed:

When he shall be judged, let him be condemned: and let his prayer become sin. . . . Let there be none to extend mercy unto him, neither let there be any to favour his fatherless children. Let his posterity be cut off; and in the generation following let their name be blotted out. (KJV)

All this and more the old man did at the behest of his religion and in the name of the God he claimed to worship.

The only redemptive thing Jacob van Vlaanderen did was to die eight days later of a stroke, which meant that at least some of his imposed restrictions could be lifted, the front door unlocked, the right of family members to be present at Pieter's trial, the possibility for relationships with some old friends to be renewed. But the mood the old man created was pervasive; Pieter's sister, long courted by the *dominee* of the church, returned his ring and would not see him again, her shame and grief outdistancing her love.

The most immediate contributor to Pieter's downfall was a fellow police-man, *Sergeant Steyn,* who had some understandable reasons to want to give Lieutenant van Vlaanderen his comeuppance. Pieter had on several occasions, during the "black moods," dealt with Steyn harshly, and humiliated him in public, thereby incurring Steyn's undying enmity. And when Steyn, almost out of the corner of his eye, intuited that something was going on between Pieter and Stephanie, he contrived, with Stephanie's collusion, to create evidence of a liaison that Pieter could not refute. It was Steyn who filed the charge, Steyn who made the public accusation, Steyn who took perverted pleasure in orchestrating the destruction of a fellow human being. Every society has its complement of such persons.

But in addition to individuals—Pieter himself, Nella, Jacob, and Steyn—the entire legal system helped to destroy Pieter. Once a charge had been made, it could not be withdrawn; the wheels of "justice" had to continue their merciless path toward destruction. The Immorality Act was looked upon as a lynchpin of Afrikaaner society. not only must the races be kept separate, they must particularly be kept sexually separate, for if not, the whole edifice of apartheid would collapse. So sexual relationships between the races were particularly vilified in South African society. On charges of breaking many other laws there might have been legal recourse, appeals, a possibility of the charges being dropped, pleas that the harshness of the sentence be mitigat-ed—but not as far as the Immorality Act was concerned.

Potential Carriers of Redemption

Throughout the story, however, there are moments when redemption might have occurred, when a breakthrough in understanding might have saved those involved from the downfall that destroyed them. And yet the moments come and go unfulfilled. There is "desolation" but no "comfort."

Tante Sophie, as narrator, is continually berating herself for not having gotten through to Pieter's inner core and given him a sense that he could trust her. For she knew that something was wrong, even if she did not know just what it was. Her narrative is laced with verbal flagellation and relentless dismay that she could not save them all, and avert their downfall. And yet, as we have noted, even when she tried most directly to break through the protective shell Pieter had created around himself, she was harshly rebuffed. Perhaps her failure was not (as she felt) that she did not try hard enough, but that she tried *too* hard, and, as she occasionally glimpsed, drove him away from her as a result. She frequently refers to the need to have "hammered on the door" of his heart even more relentlessly. But hammering was not a way to break down his defenses.

Pieter has a group of *men friends,* with all of whom he searched for ways to unburden himself, and yet at each decisive moment he could never speak the initial word; or, when he tried to speak it, they could not, or did not, hear. His friend Kappie was a source of strength to him in many ways. They shared music together, as well as a love of stamps and coffee, and Kappie was one of the few who could make the outwardly reserved Pieter smile. But appropriate occasions for deep sharing went past and could not be retrieved.

The *dominee,* new and young in the parish church, preached an initial sermon that extolled mercy as a divine attribute more fundamental than judgment, and Pieter felt, "I could talk to this man." But when the two met, the *dominee* was so overawed by meeting the famous football player van Vlaanderen, that Pieter recoiled from baring his soul. When the *dominee* asked Pieter to become a *diaken* in the church, Pieter could only respond (which was how he truly felt) that he wasn't good enough, but he could not bring himself to explain why he wasn't good enough, even in such an appropriate context. And when the *dominee* became engaged to Pieter's sister, potential channels of communication were further blocked rather than freed up.

Pieter's own superior on the police force, the *captain,* had great respect for Pieter and entrusted him with many matters. And the captain was so open and human that once—during a momentary lull in the midst of dealing with a smallpox epidemic that was leaving them little time for sleep—Pieter asked the captain if he could talk with him, and the captain, all unknowing, brushed him off by saying that if it didn't have to do with the smallpox epidemic it had better wait until morning when they had had some sleep, by which time Pieter's resolve had weakened and he invented another topic to discuss. So the matter was never shared.

Later, recalling the moment and realizing the full import of Pieter's request, the captain could only say in deep remorse at having failed Pieter, "My God, my God!" for by that time the charge had been filed and nothing could be reversed. The most he could say was, "There are terrible things to come but I'll stand by you," which he did; and to Sergeant Steyn, Pieter's betrayer, he said only, "May God forgive you for an evil deed" (p. 230).

There was even a moment when *Jacob van Vlaanderen* could have been a redeeming presence, as he in his own way sought to restore the long-broken relationship with his son. After humiliating Pieter at Kappie's store by discovering him examining stamps, Jacob later returned to the store and bought the stamps for his son. And on the day of Jacob's birthday, Pieter gave him a book about South African birds. In a gruff way the old man appeared to scorn the book—written by an Englishman!—as containing a misidentification of a phalarope, but this was his characteristically indirect way of inviting Pieter to bird-watch with him, so that they could properly identify the bird as a phalarope and prove the Englishman wrong. This they did together in a rare moment of sharing. But even this, as the title of Paton's book indicates, could not negate all the years of hostility the father had engendered, and the reconciliation did not materialize. The phalarope had come too late.

This is, indeed, a recurring message of the book. All the efforts at saving the situation come "too late," and Tante Sophie's chronicle is a recital of opportunities missed, confidences deferred, exchanges foregone, sharings postponed. Moments that might have been seized slip through fingers not grasping tightly enough. And underneath it all is surely, on everyone's part, a sense of fear—fear that the relationship is not strong enough to sustain unexpected revelations, fear that private discussions will lead to public disclosures, fear that an expression of vulnerability will be exploited.

The Word That Was Not Spoken

What could have made a difference? What could have intervened "to save us all," as Tante Sophie so frequently wondered? Paton does not spell out an answer in great detail; his book, after all, is not a sermon masquerading as a novel. But here and there are fragments in the midst of all the brokenness, fragments that taken together suggest something of the "comfort" that was not realized in the situation of "desolation."

Jacob van Vlaanderen's bottom line was condemnation, not mercy; and in this he caricatured and reversed the true center of Calvinist faith, which offers the never-ending gift of mercy. It never occurred to the father that the message of God's mercy might be the one thing most needed in the life of his son, or that human beings are themselves the vehicles through which that mercy flows. Historically, Calvinism has often gone askew at this point, Jacob van Vlaanderen being Exhibit A. And it is revealing that although the *dominee* hints at the power of mercy in his opening sermon, Paton chooses the police captain—one sworn to uphold the law and distribute judgment—to speak the most potentially healing word. To Nella's father, who has responded to the news of the disgrace of his son-in-law with the words, "I would shoot him like a dog," the captain replies, "*Meneer,* if a man takes unto himself God's right to punish, then he must also take upon himself God's promise to restore" (p. 247). The police captain is not being sentimental. Earlier, he has said to Tante Sophie, "An offender must be punished, *mejuffrou,* I don't argue about that. But to punish and not to restore, that is the greatest of all offences" (p. 246). And later to Tante Sophie, commenting on what lies ahead for Nella, he says, "There's a hard law, *mejuffrou,* that when a deep injury is done to us, we never recover until we forgive" (p. 247).

This "hard law" receives ample confirmation from old Jacob. A deep injury is, indeed, done to him, but he will not forgive; he does not recover, and eight days later he is dead.

With Pieter in custody, and his mother unequivocally forbidden by her husband to visit him in prison, Pieter's mother says some words to Tante Sophie that she may never have thought to say before in her whole lifetime, but they are strong and healing words, beyond anything Tante Sophie had ever heard from her lips:

> Say to my son, she said, that though he may suffer under the law, there is no law that can cut him off from our love, nor from the love of his friends. His life is God's, and mine and yours, and his wife's and children's, and all his friends'; and he will therefore cherish it and not despair. (p. 239)

But even as one ponders the strength and beauty of these words, one cannot but reflect: what if they had been said to Pieter before the downfall, what if they had been said many times during Pieter's upbringing, what if his mother had been able to assure him of these things when the "black moods" came—would the downfall have had to occur?

This is surely the tenor of Tante Sophie's final comment about Pieter's mother, with which the book ends, that "maybe of the power of her love that never sought itself, men would have turned to the holy task of pardon, that the body of the Lord might not be wounded twice, and virtue come of our offences" (p. 253).

I have read this book many times. On each occasion I fantasize that somehow there will be another conclusion than the one Paton has crafted. And yet I am also moved by his unwillingness to pander to my unwarranted hope, and I must finally grant the appropriateness and even the rightness of what he has written.

But if that be so, what is provided here to "persuade us to rejoice"? Not much, when measured quantitatively against many instances in the novel that offer no possible cause for rejoicing. But there are enough elusive hints of what another outcome would be like so that the book is finally elevating rather than destructive. There are moments when not only the devastating consequences of the absence of grace are noted, but the healing potential of grace is at least fleetingly present—in Nella's responsive openness to Pieter on the night of her return from a visit to her family, in the trust with which the police captain invests his relationship to Pieter, and so on. The pervasive need for grace and mercy is manifest even when it remains unrealized.

The police captain provides the clearest evidence for this conclusion in a statement we have examined in two separate parts but must now reexamine in its unity:

> An offender must be punished, *mejuffrou,* I don't argue about that. But to punish and not to restore, that is the greatest of all offences. (p. 246)

The captain is reminding Tante Sophie (and us) that we live in a moral universe in which, if we commit wrongs, we have to pay the price; we cannot "get away with it" and expect our offenses to be disregarded. It is wrong to commit an offense and expect simply to be excused and told that it doesn't matter. It does matter, and, as the captain says, "an offender must be punished." But, he continues, there is a greater offense, indeed "the greatest of all offences," and that is "to punish and not restore." Spoken to Tante Sophie, the words speak also to us.

One of the effects of tragedy as drama is to purge those who experience it—not only the participants on stage but members of the audience as well, who become more than just observers, as they vicariously participate in the events on stage. We may deplore the denouement in a tragedy, and yet as we reflect upon it we may discover that in our own case a tragic conclusion has not yet taken place, and that as a result we are empowered to approach crucial events in our own lives with deeper wisdom than we had before. And even after events that have been searing, especially when we have been guilty of offenses against God or God's children, there is the healing wisdom of Tante Sophie's final remark, that when we engage in "the holy task of pardon," virtue can come even from our offenses.

AFFIRMATION IN THE MIDST OF COMPLAINT
C. S. Lewis, *Till We Have Faces*

C. S. Lewis was a professor of English literature with theological interests and one of the most prolific writers of his generation, turning out a huge variety of books, some good, some bad, some brilliant. Lewis was least effective when trying to play the part of overt theologian. But when he turned loose his gifts of fantasy, imagination, and ingenuity, he wrote in a way that still catches readers unawares, and suddenly brings them up short with the realization that something important has been happening to them during the reading of one of his books.

A Myth Revised

There are legitimate complaints against the gods, which have been a part of human protest as long as human beings have been on the scene. In *Till We Have Faces,* Lewis voices a good many of these complaints, through a retelling of the ancient myth of Psyche (borrowed with a few changes from Ovid's *Metamorphoses*). Part I, which is at least four times as long as Part II, tells the story and recites the complaints. Part II, which is at least four times as important as Part I, revises the complaints and gives some indication of the answer of the gods to the charges. Part II is not just a moral tacked on to make things properly "religious." Rather, as the increasing self-awareness of the narrator becomes apparent, the increasing depth of the whole book, as a recital of human character in process of formation, likewise becomes apparent.

The best way to indicate the communicative power of the book will be to recall the story and see what Lewis does with it.

The purpose of the narrator, Orual, queen of Glome, is to accuse the gods. At the start of the tale her father is king, angry because he has two daughters but no son to succeed him. He takes another wife and propitiates the local deity, Ungit, in the hope of having a son. Ungit fails him (as he sees it) for a daughter is born, Istra, or Psyche. Psyche grows up in the palace with Orual and the other sister, Redival, and the three of them are taught by a Greek slave, called "the Fox," who represents Greek culture at its rational and urbane best. Psyche is beautiful, Orual is ugly, but the ugly Orual loves Psyche and is almost a mother to her, Psyche's mother having died in childbirth.

There comes a famine in the land. Psyche walks abroad and appears to the people to have the gift of healing; they look upon her as Ungit in mortal shape. But when the plague gets worse, Psyche is blamed, and instead of being called a goddess, she is now called "the Accursed." The priest of Ungit claims her as a sacrifice for Ungit, for when mortals ape the gods and steal the worship due to the gods, then the gods are angered.

No Escape from the Gods

As a result Psyche is taken to a holy place on the mountain, shackled to a sacred tree, and left to die. And here begins Orual's bitterness against the gods: first, that they took Psyche from her; second, that they did not let her have a final reconciliation with Psyche before the latter's death; and third, that Psyche was carried off gilded and painted for sacrifice in a procession in which Orual could not take part. The gods, Orual decides, are cruel and relentless:

> There is no escape from them into sleep or madness, for they can pursue you into them with dreams. Indeed you are then most at their mercy. The nearest thing we have to a defense against them (but there is no real defense) is to be very wide awake and sober and hard at work, to hear no music, never to look at earth or sky, and (above all) to love no one. (*Till We Have Faces,* pp. 88–89)

Whatever makes life good, makes one vulnerable, and exposes one to sorrow. Truly, the gods seem cruel.

Later, Orual determines that she will go up the mountain and bury Psyche's remains. She goes with Bardia, a trusted soldier, a matter-of-fact man of great common sense, who is important to Orual's later story. They find nothing at the sacrificial spot, but Bardia discovers a ruby on the ground, and beyond it they find a valley, and there, on the other side of a tiny stream . . . stands Psyche.

Orual, recovered from her shock, crosses over the stream and hears Psyche's

story. Psyche had been rescued by a god, taken to the beautiful palace in which
she is now sitting, ministered to by many servants, and is now the bride of a
god, who visits her each night, but upon whose face she may not gaze.

There is a total misunderstanding, for Orual sees no palace. She is sure that
Psyche is being tricked by someone who has built a legend of fantasy around
Psyche. She determines to rescue Psyche and bring her back to reality. But
Psyche prefers her world (which to her is obviously not make-believe) and she
loves her lover. She will not leave, even for Orual. Orual leaves, dazed, and
goes back to Glome. Just before leaving she turns around, and for a moment
she too sees the palace in all its splendor. But the picture disappears, and there
is just forest again. Did she really see it, or was she deceived?

This becomes another strand in the complaint against the gods. Why do
they not make it clear one way or the other? Was Psyche deceived, or was
Orual deceived? Why do the gods hint, rather than telling us outright? Why
don't they guide us plainly?

The momentary vision notwithstanding, Orual determines that Psyche
must be rescued. Bardia's opinion is that Psyche has been captured by a
Shadowbrute and is in the power of an evil spirit. But Bardia doesn't want to
get involved: "I think the less Bardia meddles with the gods, the less they'll
meddle with me." "The Fox" has another answer. He does not believe "the
poets' lies about the gods," and says that Psyche has been deluded by a
vagabond who is keeping her captive with the fantasy, coming under cover of
darkness so his plot will not be betrayed.

In either case—Shadowbrute or vagabond—Orual decides Psyche must be
rescued. She goes back to the mountain, and on threat of killing herself,
persuades Psyche to put her lover to the test by lighting a lamp that night and
looking at his face.

The Judgment of the Gods

Psyche does the deed and thereby brings catastrophe upon herself. The god
(for such it was) must put her out of the palace and condemn her to a life of
wandering across the earth, fulfilling well-nigh impossible tasks in penance for
her lack of trust. The god also appears to Orual, not in anger, but with
"passionless and measureless rejection. . . . He rejected, denied, answered, and
(worst of all) he knew, all I had thought, done or been." He tells her that
Psyche must go into exile, to hunger and thirst and tread hard roads, and
concludes, "You also shall be Psyche." Orual hears the weeping of Psyche,
weeping she has caused but is powerless to comfort. There is nothing for
Orual to do but return home and await her own destruction.

But destruction does not come. Orual returns to Glome and decides that she will go veiled, as a kind of treaty with her ugliness, and also, one suspects, as a kind of penance enacted by one upon whose face a god has looked in judgment. Rather than being doomed to die, she is doomed to live. She becomes queen and is a good and efficient queen. She becomes expert with the sword, and legends grow up about her, particularly after she defeats Prince Argan in mortal combat. Hers is a reign of peace, prosperity, and progress.

After the death of "the Fox," Orual goes on a journey that opens up a wound she had almost healed by years of busyness. In a distant land she discovers a temple to a new goddess, Istra. The priest of Istra tells her Psyche's story, and from Orual's perspective tells it all wrong. He tells of a sister who saw the palace of Psyche, was jealous, and brought about Psyche's downfall, condemning her to wander the face of the world, treading hard roads.

This is the last straw. Orual decides to write down her charges against the gods, for in this charge that she was jealous of Psyche is proof that the gods have not only laughed at her but spat in her face. She must expose them. For if the gods had revealed themselves clearly, and not ambiguously, there would have been no need for a sad tale about Psyche. Orual demands "a different world, a world in which the gods show themselves clearly," and in which they do not torment human beings "with glimpses, nor unveil to one what they hide from another, nor ask you to believe what contradicts your eyes and ears and nose and tongue and fingers" (p. 253).

Here, then, is the final, culminating charge against the gods, a stirring, human indictment:

They gave me nothing in the world to love but Psyche and then took her away from me. But that was not enough. They then brought me to her at such a place and time that it hung on my word whether she should continue in bliss or be cast out into misery. They would not tell me whether she was the bride of a god, or mad, or a brute's or villain's spoil. *They would give no clear sign,* though I begged for it. I had to guess. And because I guessed wrong they punished me; what's worse, punished me through her . . . . I say the gods deal very unrightly with us. For they will neither (which would be best of all) go away and leave us to live our own short days to ourselves, nor will they show themselves openly to us and tell us what they would have us do. For that too would be endurable. But to hint and hover, to draw near us in dreams and oracles, or in a waking vision that vanishes as soon as seen, to be dead silent when we question them and then glide back and whisper (words we cannot understand) in our ears when we most wish to be free of them, and to show to one what they hide from another; what is all this but cat-and-mouse play, blindman's bluff and mere jugglery? Why must holy places be dark places?

I say, therefore, that there is no creature (toad, scorpion, or serpent) so noxious to man as the gods. Let them answer my charges if they can. It may well be that instead of answering, they'll strike me mad or leprous or turn me into beast, bird, or tree. But will not all the world then know (and the gods will know it knows) that this is because they have no answer? (pp. 258–259, italics added)

End of Part I. End, presumably, of the complaint against the gods. Orual has voiced not only her own complaint, but the timeless complaint of all the ages against the gods: Why do they give no clear sign? Why do they hint and hover? Why won't they simply leave us alone? Why won't they show themselves openly?

The Force of the Complaint

If Lewis offers much corroboration here to the nonbeliever, he offers little reassurance to the believer. It is not possible for the latter to say, "But all that has been taken care of. God *has* given us a clear sign in Jesus of Nazareth."

The response is too glib. For the claim about a divine incarnation only heightens rather than lessens the intensity of the complaint. Christ does *not* make it "a sure thing." His revelation does *not* reveal fully, totally, transparently. It too can be rejected, denied, dismissed as illusion, just as Orual dismissed Psyche's palace. Why should we believe that God has become incarnate in a carpenter's son? Why should we look for God among, of all places, the Jews? Why should we expect to find divine love in the midst of the shame, the filth, and the obscenity of a first-century crucifixion? Orual's complaint is not one that can be disposed of by pointing to the God of Christian faith. Indeed, it can be argued that claims on behalf of the God of Christian faith force us to rewrite Orual's complaint in italics.

There is, however, an answer given to Orual. Part of the answer involves a redrafting of the complaint. It comes in visions and hints, but it *is* an answer.

No sooner has Orual set down her story than she realizes it is not her full story. She has been very selective. She has written in a way that will show her in the most favorable light. But other interpretations of her story, which she thought she had successfully dealt with, come crowding back to the surface. The writing of the complaint was "only to prepare me for the gods' surgery. They used my own pen to probe my wound" (p. 263). She discovers, for example, that she sinned against Redival, the sister whom she disliked, by disregarding her through all their growing up. In giving herself so totally to Psyche's upbringing, Orual had created a terrible and twisted knot in Redival's heart. For years, Orual realizes now, she had "used" Bardia, drawing so heavily on his time and energy that Bardia's home life had been ruined. She wore him out with the demands of state and directly caused his premature death.

Such reassessments of her life force her to reassess the gods as well. Ungit, for example. In a dream, it becomes clear to Orual that in a real sense she *is* Ungit, "gorged with men's stolen lives." The discovery is overpowering. She determines to drown herself. She goes to the river, straps her ankles together and is about to throw herself in, when a voice, the voice of a god, says, "Do not do it" (p. 190). There is no rebellion left in her, and she does not drown herself.

Very well, being Ungit, and thus ugly in soul, she must change her ugly soul into a fair one. This she determines to do, the gods being her helpers. But how can one, by the mere willing of it, change an ugly soul into a fair one? It cannot be done, not even for thirty minutes at a stretch, as she bitterly discovers: "I could mend my soul no more than my face. Unless the gods helped. And why did the gods not help?" (p. 293).

Another vision: She is in a field. The gods' rams are running through the field, and a single golden fleck from their sides will make her beautiful in soul. But as she approaches them to claim the gift, they trample her down. She sees a woman in another part of the field picking up flecks of gold that the rams have left in the thorns during their charge on Orual: "She won without effort what utmost effort would not win for me" (p. 295). So Orual cannot work her way into a more satisfactory relationship with the gods. Even the best intentions are insufficient.

The Real Complaint

In another vision she is led to a judgment hall where she can once more voice her complaint. She stands naked before the court. There will be no pretense here.

And at this point the *real* complaint against the gods comes out with devastating clarity. The earlier complaint, the one we all make, was not the true complaint. We use it as a device to hide the real nature of our complaint against the gods. For the real complaint, Orual discovers, is one of jealousy. The gods are our rivals. They take the ones we love best.

She complains to the gods with a new level of bitter intensity:

> It would be far better for us if you were foul and ravening. We'd rather you drank their blood than stole their hearts. We'd rather they were ours and dead than yours and made immortal. But to steal her love from me, to make her see things I couldn't see. . . . There's no room for you and us in the same world. You're a tree in whose shadow we can't thrive. We want to be our own. . . . What should I care for some horrible, new happiness which I hadn't given her and which separated her from me? Do you think I wanted her to be happy that way? . . . Do you ever remember whose the girl was? She was mine. *Mine;* do you not know what the word means? Mine! You're thieves, seducers." (pp. 302–303)

This is a different matter. This is the real complaint. If we found it easy to identify with Orual's earlier complaint, we are less prepared to do so with this one. We are prepared to be sophisticated about our doubts, but to concede that they come from bitterness at the extent to which the divine interferes with life—that is something we would prefer to examine no further.

But Orual *has* examined further and voiced her bitterest objections. She who was "faceless" for so many years with the wearing of the veil, has now been stripped in body and soul, the veil across her entire life removed. And as she herself can confess, "The complaint was the answer. To hear myself making it was to have been answered" (p. 305). She has finally been forced to utter the speech that had lain at the center of her soul for years. She discovered that what we *really are* must be "dug out of us" before we can face the gods.

> I saw well why the gods do not speak to us openly, nor let us answer. Till that word can be dug out of us [the word that says who we truly are] why should they hear the babble that we think we mean? How can they meet us face to face till we have faces? (p. 305)

The gods will give answers only to honest charges. As long as we are faceless, superficial, hypocritical, or sophisticated, they will not deal with us. Our words can form a barrier to our understanding. Even Orual's tutor, "the Fox" (dead but present at the judgment) understands this and sees that it has been his sin to substitute words for reality, maxims for truth, philosophy for transforming power.

Beyond Justice

But Orual's judgment is not yet over, although her insight has certainly increased. "The Fox" takes her further on, consoling her with the thought that at least she "will not get justice." The gods (thank God) are not just, for "what would become of us if they were?" (p. 308). There must be a salvation beyond justice. And there is.

"The Fox" takes Orual to a place where she has a revision of her previous visions. Orual sees someone by a river, strapping her ankles, about to jump in and drown. It is Psyche. "Do not do it," Orual calls to the picture, and Psyche unties her ankles and goes away. Orual sees Psyche approaching a field to get some golden wool from the gods' rams. Psyche cannot get near them, but suddenly the rams turn upon another intruder and trample her down. As they charge, flecks of fleece come off on the thorns, and Psyche gleans them without effort.

So it goes. Psyche, Orual, Orual, Psyche. The one helping the other. The other helping the one. At times, in her travels, Psyche seems almost happy. "The Fox" explains that it is because "Another bore nearly all the anguish." The "other" was Orual. Orual bore the anguish, Psyche achieved the tasks. "The Fox" asks almost mockingly, "Would you rather have had justice?"

Here is a theme writ large across human history, the theme of substituted love, of men and women—and gods—taking upon one another the bearing of burdens too great to be borne alone. Psyche bore much for Orual, through her wandering and toil and anguish, and Orual, without knowing it, bore much for Psyche. "She bore much love for you then," "the Fox" tells Orual. "You have borne something for her since." It is clear that Lewis is here drawing upon his friend, Charles Williams, whose theme of "the practice of substituted love" was discussed in an earlier chapter.

Psyche and Orual finally meet face to face. Pictures and images and visions are now over. There need be no more deception, and Orual can now say in utter honesty, "I never wished you well, never had one selfless thought of you. I was a craver." But since the bearing of burdens can work both ways and must be reciprocal, more happens than merely the recognition of the past. As Orual has borne part of the pain for Psyche so that Psyche can accomplish the tasks set before her, now Orual is made beautiful as a result of the tasks Psyche has accomplished. Psyche's journeys have led her to that which will remake Orual into a thing of beauty. Orual looks into the pool and sees two Psyches, both beautiful. The great voice that had once said a dreadful word to her, "You also are Psyche," now says a blessed word to her: "You also are Psyche." She is in the presence of the god, and the presence is one not of judgment but of mercy. She has heard the glad news, the only truly redeeming and transforming news: "the Divine Nature can change the past."

The "Answer"

Part I had ended with the words "no answer." The gods can give no answer to the charges we bring against them. But when the true nature of the charges has been exposed, and we see ourselves as we truly are (and thus begin to see the gods as they truly are), the entire situation is changed:

> I know now, Lord, why you utter no answer. You are yourself the answer.
> Before your face questions die away. What other answer would suffice? (p. 319)

"How can the gods meet us face to face till we have faces?" Orual asked earlier in her judgment. They cannot, or at least will not. But when the veil is stripped away, God seems to be the answer. "I had heard of thee by the hearing of the ear," said another Orual at another time, likewise making complaint against the gods, "but now mine eye seeth thee." And that, for Orual, for Job, and perhaps even for us—is enough.

The complaint against the gods sounds reasonable until we recognize that it is not our real complaint but an evasion of our real complaint. And for those who enter vicariously with Orual into the real complaint that is made without a veil, it may be that there can be granted vicariously to us the salvation that came to her.

10

SAINTHOOD IN THE MIDST OF EARTHINESS
Frederick Buechner, *Brendan*

Frederick Buechner has a deservedly high reputation as a contemporary writer, author of a dozen novels and eleven books of nonfiction at the latest tally, one of his recent novels, *Godric,* having been a Pulitzer Prize nominee. Most of the novels have contemporary settings, *Godric* and *Brendan* being the exceptions, and the nonfiction includes autobiographical volumes, collections of sermons and essays, a book on the use of literary genres in preaching, and deftly handled treatments of biblical characters and theological definitions.

We are not, in other words, dealing with just any old contemporary writer, but with that *rara avis,* a writer of distinction who is also a theologian. A full Buechner vita would even reveal that he is an ordained Presbyterian minister.

This accumulation of credentials will be an initial hindrance to some and an invitation to others. There are pitfalls either way. Sceptics or agnostics will be suspicious that Buechner is only a kind of evangelist-for-the-thinking-person, whose writing is bent to nefarious ends like conversion, while believers will anticipate entering a realm in which faith will be made easy because an intellectual has taken the time to fashion crutches for the less adept. Both assumptions are in error because they assume an incorrect starting point. The correct starting point is that Buechner is first and last a *writer,* and what entices one to read him is that he brings perspectives to his work that are not shared by most of his fellow artisans.

This needs amplification.

It helps to know where writers are coming from, even though there is ample evidence that the most impeccable theological credentials cannot ensure good writing in general or expertise in the novelist's craft in particular. Suffice it to say, then, that Buechner is not a "theological novelist," as though the adjective adorned the noun, but rather a novelist who also happens to be a theologian. This does not mean that his novels will demonstrate the efficacy of belief, or provide sugar coating for a variety of bitter theological pills; it simply means that in Buechner's dealing with life—assuredly the novelist's province—a theological perspective can be discerned. This does not reduce the novels to propaganda; it merely means that among the forces at work in human lives, the struggle between belief and unbelief will be part of the mix, and if you are a theologian as well as a writer you have some things to contribute to the mix that other writers don't have, provided—a most important proviso—you refrain from stacking the deck. Buechner is an implacable foe of deck stacking. *Brendan* is a case in point.

First off, and most important, it is a rousing tale, broad and even bawdy at times, about a sixth-century Irish priest who dedicated his life to voyaging the seas in a precarious craft to seek Tir-na-n-Og, the "land of the blessed," the place where sixth-century Celts felt sure the departed went after death. Brendan's travels became the stuff of legends, and Buechner has seized on the available historical facts to weave a piece of fiction that may, like all good fiction, be "truer than the facts."

The tale is told by Finn, Brendan's lifelong friend and chronicler. Finn is the kind of functionary every man hankering for sainthood, or for reaching Tir-na-n-Og ahead of his allotted time, needs to guide him through the paths and pitfalls of an earthly vale of tears. Finn writes in sixth-century style, includes enough sixth-century miracles to make his tale credible, and charms us with such literary gems as a version of Psalm 23 that goes, "Christ is my druid, I shall want for nothing . . . he cloaks me in a thick mist from the eyes of my enemies! He reads the secrets of my heart like the guts of an owl!" (p. 82). Finn's description of the wild events of Brendan's life before the voyages begin (too numerous for discussion in a précis), the voyages themselves, the storms, the islands visited, the strange people encountered, the bizarre episodes along the way, keep the reader enchanted, even while it is becoming apparent that the inner voyage of Brendan's soul is the real subject of the tale.

And that inner voyage, far from being tame by comparison, is even more tempestuous than the outer one, albeit the two cannot be neatly disentangled, since neither makes sense without the other.

Brendan embarks twice on a quest for "the land of the blessed," and Finn misses the first trip, being unceremoniously washed overboard in a storm just as the currach is leaving port. So Brendan gives us the first account himself. There are wild adventures, particularly with whales and volcanoes, the loss of a companion overboard, a convincing apparition of Judas still doing penance for "the kissing of a friend by moonlight," a curse against God by one of the companions, and a final arrival at what they take to be Tir-na-n-Og. But "the land of the blessed" turns out to have shrunken human heads resting on flat stones, and little children on the beach "playing at coupling."

This denouement sobers Brendan, who decides to spend his time in the land of the still living, organizing communities of monks, building a convent for some nuns, as well as pulling off a miracle now and then. An order to a subordinate results in the death of a monk, and a monk who survived, Malo, becomes a thorn in Brendan's flesh, and vice versa.

An elderly nun finally persuades Brendan once again to seek "the land of the blessed," this time in a stouter boat, but with Malo taken along as penance, so the two of them can work at the ill will that has persistently deepened between them. And then, "for strengthening your heart against hard times to come," the nun bares her breast and he takes milk "rich and sweet as Heaven." Such is the stuff of sixth-century Celtic spirituality.

The story mounts in a crescendo in the final two sections, "The Land of the Blessed" and "The Sentence of the Judge." During a second voyage, the tensions between Brendan and Malo deepen; it turns out Malo had wanted to die in place of the monk who did, and Brendan had, inadvertently, saved him. Unfinished business between them remains.

Land is finally sighted, and whether or not it is Tir-na-n-Og remains in doubt through a series of episodes that confirm at least that if it does exist Tir-na-n-Og is several complicated days' journey inland. The available directions have been exhausted by the time the seekers reach a wide river. The recurring and burning question: does "the land of the blessed" lie on the far side?

And here, within reach of his heart's desire (if his heart's desire *does* lie on the far shore), Brendan pauses and—in an extraordinary twist for a quest story—elects not to find out. With piercing clarity, Finn surveys Brendan's options:

> Suppose the King of Heaven himself was waiting there with all the others to welcome him? That would be nothing to sneeze at surely, but could it be Brendan fancied more just the whiff of Heaven you get in the salt breeze sometimes or in the glimpse of it in a whale's eye? He was always one for teasing the heathens like that anyhow. He'd give them a peek through the pearly gates

every now and then but never knock them silly with the whole grand glory of it
at a clap.

   Suppose the King of Heaven didn't welcome him at all? Could it be Brendan
feared he'd curse him for his sins instead and send him off to a rock in the sea like
Judas or the fiery mountain of Hell?

   Suppose he got across somehow and found the far shore of the river was only
the far shore of the river, no worse and no better than the shore he was on?

   Suppose not even there could Maeve [the resident sceptic] make out so much
as the print of God's shoe? (p. 197)

Suppose the proof lay right there across the water. Did he really want
proof? Wasn't faith something that could never be claimed as a sure thing,
without taking the glory out of it? Suppose the verdict on his life was
judgment rather than blessedness? No need to find out just yet if that was to be
his fate. Suppose there was nothing there but more of the same? Suppose,
finally, there was nothing there for Maeve? Then why make the fording?

So, turning his back on a quest so near completion—one way or the
other—Brendan settles for scooping up black muck from the riverbed to
annoint a dying companion with the sign of the cross, and death, not life, is
the end result of the quest for Tir-na-n-Og.

Was this cowardice on Brendan's part, or at best timidity, in the face of a
monumental choice? I think it was courage, and the first consideration
outweighed the other three in gravity. Things are not tied up neatly in this life,
and the notion that we can force the hand of destiny and read our own story
clear and unvarnished ahead of time is asking for what we cannot have, and in
the deepest sense *do not want*. If between two humans, love is measured only
by the degree of its "provability," then love has been absent from the equation
from the start. And Brendan discovers that the same thing is true between
himself and God. Such love is measured by commitment, risk, and sharing,
not by a demand for quantifiable data.

Which isn't the end of the story. For what do you do with the rest of your
life if its previously single-minded focus suddenly goes blurry? What is ahead
if you come back from a grand quest empty-handed? So on his return Brendan
is "at sea" in a way he had never been when he was handling the tiller in a gale.

Chiefly he is guilt-ridden that his obsessive voyages have cost a lot of lives,
and he feels the burden of responsibility for the deaths of Crossan, Dismas,
Gestas, and other companions who died because of his misdirected zeal. The
voyages, he decides, "never did anybody a bit of good least of all Christ"
(p.206). So he becomes a recluse, more and more shutting himself off from
the world, trying by penitential acts to set the ledger right. By a design finally
of Brendan's own choosing, Malo becomes his confessor, and pouring out his

sins to one who has hated him begins in a curious way to establish bonds between the two.

But then comes an event—not at all of Brendan's own choosing—that results in a change of direction and initiates the redemption of his aggrieved soul. Brigit, a nun, visits Brendan in his fastness and starts to work in him a change so great that Finn, chronicling it, compares her to Jesus bringing forth Lazarus from the grave, since by her act Brendan is restored to life out of living death. There is no breast baring in this encounter between nun and priest, just good sound advice and a bit of scolding. Brigit tells him he was "never cut out for this sort of monkishness" (p. 210), and exhorts him to leave his island cell and go out among the people—people who need help, who need encouragement, who need love, who need Christ. Brendan, in his own need, must be willing both to give and to receive: "Bring Christ to them, Brendan, and in God's good time perhaps they'll bring him again to you" (p. 211). Christ will surely not be found in isolation from other humans; Christ can perhaps be found in interchange with other humans.

So Brendan sets out on another quest, if he had known enough to call it that. He finds a clarifying counterfoil in Gildas, a monk who is frenetically keeping a chronicle of all the iniquities of the region, so that, come the day of judgment, nobody will slip through the fingers of God and make it to heaven on the cheap. As Brendan and Gildas debate the will of heaven about such matters, words are drawn from Brendan that are new. God, he tells Gildas, "wants us each one to have a loving heart. . . . When all's said and done, perhaps that's the length and breadth of it" (p. 216). Exit Gildas, unimpressed, to resume entries in his chronicle under such headings as *Peccatores, Adulteri, Fornicarii*.

But good comes out of this encounter between Brendan (convinced that he has misspent his life), Finn (disturbed that he had left his wife in order to serve Brendan), and Gildas (who has but one sound leg). For when Gildas stumbles during his departure, Brendan reaches out and saves him from a bad fall. And Finn comments, "We was cripples all of us. . . . 'To lend each other a hand when we're falling,' Brendan said, 'Perhaps that's the only thing that matters in the end' " (p. 217).

So there begins a new work for Brendan, sent him from heaven he believes, the day he caught the stumbling Gildas: "to lend each other a hand when we're falling." He sees it as a different kind of penance for all the time he'd spent running away from folks by means of his voyages, "when he'd better have been caring after the naked and hungry and sick at home" (p. 219).

Small deeds dot the landscape of the rest of his life, but they are deeds that

give meaning to apparently inconsequential lives—and occasionally to consequential lives as well, for there is an encounter with King Arthur at Caerlon,
who needed peace as much as anyone, his life having crumbled when his wife
and best friend betrayed him. There was even a war Brendan stopped by
praying up a mist so thick the armies finally gave up trying to find one another
and went home.

When Brendan died he was still in fear of "the sentence of the judge." But
Finn, the unsophisticated Finn, was naive enough to suggest what sentence he
would pass, were he the heavenly judge: "I'd sentence him to have mercy on
himself. I'd sentence him less to strive for the glory of God than just to let it
swell his sails if it can" (p. 240). But whatever God's judgment, Finn's own
judgment was clear: "I'd tell him he has my pardon anyhow" (p. 240).

In any telling of it apart from Buechner's own text, there is a danger that the
latter sections of the book will sound too homiletical, as though the whole tale
had become one long sermon. But Buechner's craft saves him from such a
charge, and the twist in the quest emerges as one that, while surprising at first,
leads the reader on subsequent reflection to say, "Of course!" and then
perhaps to muse: where, if we cannot successfully flee humankind, shall we
find meaning save in the service of humankind? Or else to muse: if the price of
seeking God is to desert God's children, and so render the quest unprofitable,
the only genuine alternative will be to turn to serve God's children, hoping
that, out of the corner of one's eye, there may be an occasional glimpse of God
in their midst.

11

STRENGTH IN THE MIDST OF PAIN
Alice Walker,
The Color Purple

In what is more than a flight of fancy, Alice Walker describes how the characters in her books become so real to her that on days when the writing is going well (or badly) they visit her in the afternoons, commenting on the words she has been putting in their mouths, challenging or approving the course of the plot development, and raising other kindred subjects in which they have a vested interest. At the end of *The Color Purple,* she thanks them all for help rendered and identifies herself in two roles: as the *author* who crafts the material and as the *medium* through whom the material is transmitted. The writing process, she claims elsewhere, is "a visitation of spirits." The fact that her characters assume a stubborn independence, which she can "mediate" but not control, argues for their authenticity. Characters are not introduced simply to be passive transmitters of the author's viewpoint; they are endowed with freedom—freedom to be themselves and if necessary to defy their creator, who, in giving them freedom, has voluntarily circumscribed a measure of her own freedom for their sakes.

We can use this perspective as an analogy for the freedom of human beings in relation to God the creator, as Dorothy Sayers demonstrated in a book from an earlier era, *The Mind of the Maker.* Both the human creator (the author) and the divine Creator (God) have to play by the rules of the game. Truly to grant freedom to one's creation means entering into a contract with integrity, so that the creatures can truly defy the creator's will, if they feel called to do so, and exert their own wills.

There are, of course, ground rules for the creatures as well: they must be willing to accept the consequences of their autonomous actions, which, if working at cross-purposes to the will of their creator, have the possible consequence of getting them into trouble. They accept that possible consequence, for to be free creatures rather than automatons is always to be preferred. The creators, for their part (whether human or divine), can see this whole scheme as a plus, for without a clash of wills, whether between creatures or between creatures and their creator, any plot is going to be drab.

Alice Walker's relation, as a creature in her own right, to the Creator of all, has been partially shaped by her own experiences. A black woman, she grew up in the South during the civil rights era, with its times of marches, protests, sit-ins, civil disobedience, jail sentences, and occasional lynchings. She was exposed to many versions of the church's relationship to these events, a few of which were consistent with the gospel, but many of which were complicit in strengthening forces of evil rather than challenging and subduing them. But whatever the state of organized religion, the power and depth of the religious impulse is ever present in Alice Walker's writings, nowhere more fully than in her Pulitzer Prize–winning novel, *The Color Purple*.

Breaking Down Boundaries

Although there are some classic instances of black-white confrontations within the book—"classic" in the sense that whites tend to win the power struggle and blacks tend to lose—the deeper dynamics of the book center on intramural struggles between black people themselves, usually poor, and possessed of their own share of human foibles.

In light of this, it is a tribute to the author, and to the characters for whom she is a self-appointed "medium," that a cast of predominantly black characters confronts many white, middle-class readers with people to whom they can relate strongly, facing problems and decisions that are the stuff of all human experience. I have frequently used *The Color Purple* in college and seminary courses made up predominantly of white, middle-class students, and can testify to the degree that Alice Walker confronts them on the deepest levels of their own being. This is especially true with women students who, whatever their racial and social background, feel deep kinship with Celie and her struggle for liberation.

Consider the world from which Celie seeks liberation. It is

. . . a world where women can routinely expect to be raped, inside and
      outside of marriage;

. . . a world where there is no expectation of "equal justice before the law";

. . . a world where role expectations for women and men are rigidly enough
defined so that any breach is dangerous;

. . . a world where casual sex, devoid of love, is the norm;

. . . a world where religion is usually escapist;

. . . a world where there are almost no escape routes from grinding poverty,
and where economic powerlessness translates into political powerlessness;

. . . a world where one dare not express the full extent of the rage and pain
that have been building up through a lifetime;

. . . a world where people are not characterized as selves, but as members of
a group or class;

. . . a world where the most one can ever expect are small victories, never
secure and almost never cumulative.

Such problems as these—and many more—are central to the characters in
The Color Purple. And yet any honest examination of the world of Alice
Walker's fiction makes us aware that the same problems are increasing rather
than diminishing, not only in our inner cities and our poverty-stricken rural
areas, but in the middle-class world as well.

This suggests the possibility that communication and conscientization
across rigidly divided sectors of our society might be more possible than we
had previously assumed, and that with a guide—or "medium"—as capable as
Alice Walker, we might be able to learn from one another. We can test this
proposition by examining two threads in her novel: a compressed exchange
about God between Celie and Shug, and a tracing of the long road from
alienation to friendship traveled by Celie and Mr. ——— .

Celie and Shug

The exchange between Celie, narrator of the story, and Shug, a colorful,
flamboyant, deeply caring bisexual woman, is concentrated in a few pages.[1] It
is significant that Shug is a "messenger" of good news—which is one way to
define an "angel"—for Shug is not one on whom the strictures of conventional
morality weigh heavily, particularly when it comes to sex. Fortunately for us,
however, conventional purity is seldom the hallmark of those who impart
wisdom to us, else we would remain spiritually immature if not illiterate.

Celie has given up writing letters to God, as she had been doing since the
first page of the novel. Her repudiation has been definitive; when Shug refers
to God, Celie expresses total indifference. In response to Celie's question
about what God has possibly done in her life, Shug itemizes Celie's blessings
as life, health, and someone who loves her, i.e., Shug herself.

But Celie can do some itemizing of her own in response to her assessment of what God has given her, and the inventory includes a father who was lynched, a mother who was crazy, a stepfather who was brutal, and a sister who could have made a difference but is unavailable. When Shug, genuinely shocked, admonishes Celie to lower her voice in case God hears, Celie has a ready response: if God had ever taken the trouble to listen to poor black women, the world would be a considerably better place.

Shug acknowledges that while belief is hard, so is disbelief; it is not easy, trying to live without God, and even if one is sure that God isn't there, trying to live without God is stressful, to say the least. Shug had worried a lot about God in the past, but two important discoveries have altered her viewpoint. First discovery: to feel that God loves us makes us want to please God through things that please us. Second discovery: the first discovery is liberating rather than enslaving. It doesn't mean a dutiful round of churchgoing, choir singing, or even feeding the preacher after the service. All that is optional, left to the will and discretion of the believer. Shug's own response is to be freed up; she can relax, enjoy the world around her, and have a great time just living.

To Celie, untutored in theological niceties of such a captivating sort, Shug's program sounds like blasphemy. But Shug presses her case: people don't find God in church. They may go to church, hoping that God will put in an appearance, but basically people *bring* God to church, where they share the God they know rather than hoping to encounter some other God for the first time.

Shug elicits from Celie an image of God that fits all the conventional stereotypes: the old man with a beard and bluish-gray eyes who is not only white but wears white robes and goes barefoot. This is the same God in whom Shug once believed—a God extracted from the white Christian Bible, in which blacks are under a curse. And Shug has long ago concluded that any God who is white and male is an expendable item in her universe.

What has revived her interest is a new belief that God is not "out there" somewhere, but inside us all, and part of everything that is. Her journey back to a faith of her own has moved from the bearded old white man to nature (trees, air, and birds) and then to other people. And before the erudite reader can mutter "panentheism," Shug's catalogue of places where God is found has been enlarged to include the realm of sex.

Once again Celie feels the hovering presence of blasphemy, not only, we can be sure, because such a conviction goes beyond whatever conventional morality she had absorbed in a hectic upbringing, but because (as the reader knows full well by page 178) her sexual experience has never been anything but ugly, exploitive, painful, and rapacious. But Shug is now in full gear: Sex is just about the best thing God ever dreamed up, and the fact that God made it means that it isn't dirty or demeaning. The theme expands: God has given us not only sex but *all* the wonders of the world, and our job is simply to be a part of it all and admire it. God, rather than asking for kudos, simply wants to share the whole with us; indeed, God is angered when we pass a field full of the color purple and pay no heed. When we try to please God, Shug believes, God wants to please us back and offers us gifts when we least expect them. If she had known the adjective, Shug could have had a verbal field day reporting on the serendipitous God.

By this time, Celie is beginning to get tuned in: Can it be that God also wants to be loved? Shug responds fervently that everything and everyone wants to be loved. This opens up new possibilities for Celie, the chief of which is the possibility of wonder. Things aren't too clear yet, for the bearded white man still lurks in the wings, and she has never thought much about the amazing world that a new kind of God provides. New questions emerge: How does corn grow? Where does purple come from? What are wildflowers? There's a universe out there waiting to be noticed, a whole creation waiting to be admired, and most important of all, folks waiting to be loved. (In addition, there is a lot of evil to be challenged; rock-throwing could destroy some idols and belongs high on the agenda.)

By the end of the book, Celie is ready once again to address a letter to God, but, thanks to Shug, it is a very different God from the God of the first letter, for to address God now is also to address (as she does) the stars, the trees, the people, everything. For God is in everything.

Celie and Mr. ——

But all the way through Celie's life there has been a terrible burden: the man to whom she was married off by her stepfather, a man she so dislikes that she cannot, until very near the end of the book, even condescend to use his name, referring to him simply as Mr. ——. Observing the shifts in this relationship will reveal much about Alice Walker's sense of the degree of redemption possible even for humanity's most troubled participants.

Celie is "married off" to Mr. —— simply because he needs someone to take care of his children and household. It is a marriage of convenience, if we understand by that term a marriage for *his* convenience. Celie is his second choice. His first choice is Celie's older sister, Nettie. But the stepfather says no to that proposal, and Mr. —— has to settle for what is left. He is not the least bit enthusiastic about what is left until the stepfather offers to throw in a cow to make the deal more palatable, and even then enthusiasm does not cloud Mr.

———'s vision. It is a straightforward business transaction—a transfer of ownership between two men, the commodity in question being a woman.

After the marriage, Mr. ——— continues to have eyes for Nettie, and in his frustration at her rebuffs takes to beating Celie. When Nettie leaves, going eventually to Africa as a missionary, Mr. ———, still angered that he never got his way with her, vows to her that he will keep the two sisters apart, which he does for years by intercepting the letters Nettie writes to Celie from Africa. He is so successful that Celie does not even know the cause of her deprivation until she and Shug, almost by accident, discover a huge cache of Nettie's letters hidden in a trunk upstairs. The deception not only wounds Celie but angers her so deeply that she would surely have killed Mr. ——— microseconds after the discovery had it not been for the moderating influence of Shug.

Long before that, an incident had indicated the extent of estrangement between them. Mr. ———'s father visits the house and is particularly spiteful both to his son and daughter-in-law. Celie writes poignantly that the moment of their joint castigation brought them closer to one another than they had ever been before. So it remains throughout most of the book, Celie being verbally abused, sexually assaulted, and treated as trash.

Only after the freeing conversation with Shug about God do things begin to change. Shug announces one mealtime that not only is she leaving the household but she is taking Celie with her. Mr. ——— has no resources for handling such an announcement. Who *are* these women to think that they can spite his will? But women are getting liberated all around the dining room table: Squeak, Harpo's wife, announces that she, too, will leave—the same Squeak who has demanded in vain that she be called by her real name, Mary Agnes, since only as Mary Agnes has she been freed up enough to think well of herself and to sing.

As the women are leaving, Mr. ——— unleashes a barrage of invective at Celie, concentrating mainly on her physical unattractiveness; she is ugly and skinny and strangely shaped. But Celie, rapidly emerging from her psychic cocoon, begins to give as good as she gets. To everyone's surprise, including her own, she aggressively lays a curse on Mr. ———, the sum and substance of which is that he is going to be called upon to pay for all the evil he has done. Celie does not know quite how it is happening—words keep coming out of her mouth that seem to have been shaped elsewhere. But the hurts of a lifetime, submerged within her, finally surface and are acknowledged. It is the beginning of a cleansing.

Later Celie returns for a funeral. She notices that Mr. ——— appears to be changing. He is cleaner than before. He seems to have had a hard time. He is working harder (something Celie finds particularly hard to believe, considering his track record of sloth over a lifetime). He appears fearful when Celie appears, a reaction she not unnaturally cherishes for the moment.

One reason that accounts for the change is that Harpo, his son, has made Mr. —— turn over all the remaining letters from Nettie, and this seems to have been a catalyst for moral purging, the event out of which his life begins to move in a new direction. A deed of *caring* is beginning to detoxify the air.

Later, when Celie is feeling low, she writes to Nettie that of all those around her, Mr. —— alone has some sense of what she is going through. When he says he realizes that she hates him for keeping Nettie's letters hidden from her, she can write to Nettie that she doesn't hate him, and for two significant reasons. First, he loves Shug, and Celie also loves Shug; second, there was a time when Shug loved him. The shared love of a third person is drawing the two of them closer to each other. A circle akin to love is widening; a circle akin to hate is diminishing.

To this new situation is added something even newer, the emergence of *honesty*. Celie and Mr. —— have a number of exchanges characterized by truth-telling. Mr. —— can acknowledge that Celie's love for Shug is not surprising because he too has loved Shug all his life. He tells Celie that he told Shug that the reason he beat Celie was because she was Celie and not Shug, and he resented Celie. Celie is able to handle this. And when she confesses to Mr. —— that she had told Shug about Mr. —— 's beatings in the first place, he shares the fact that Shug defended Celie to him, accusing him of beating someone she loves.

Honesty helps to clear the air, and leads the way toward *trust*. After Shug objects to Mr. ——'s beating of Celie, Mr. —— confesses that he would like to have killed Celie. When he sees that Shug and Celie are very close, and are now separated by many miles, he can even acknowledge that he is sorry Shug left her, since he remembers how it was when Shug left him.

Truth and honesty continue to deepen. Celie reports a further conversation with Mr. —— in which he acknowledges how long it took to discover that she was really good company, and Celie can realize that while he's not Shug, he is at least someone she can talk to freely.

And then the *wonder* to which Shug had begun to introduce Celie in their conversation about God becomes an increasing part of Celie's and Mr. ——'s relationship. He reports that his inability to raise his children just about broke his heart, and Celie replies with considerable maturity that if he is sorry in his heart he is not quite as outcast as he imagines. And this unleashes a series of remarkable reflections on wonder by Mr. ——.

To start with one question, he realizes, is to end up with fifteen. Why do we need love? Why do we suffer? Why are we black? Why are we men and women? Where do children really come from? To think about such things is to realize how little we really know. We can ask all the questions, but they fall before the really important question: Why are we here?

Celie wants to know how he answers the really important question. And Mr. —— has an answer, which is that we are here to wonder, to ask questions. The more we ask about big things the more we learn, almost by chance, about the little things. We don't learn more about the big things than we start with, but the more we keep wonder alive, the more we keep love alive as well.

Celie proposes that it goes both ways: If you love, people will begin to love you back. And Mr. —— concurs.

All of that enhances the ability to *share*. Shug returns for a visit, and sees a little purple frog on the mantelpiece. (Frogs have played an important part in some of Celie's less-than-flattering comparisons between Mr. —— and members of the frog kingdom.) Shug wonders about the frog, and Celie plays it cool: It's just a small gift that Mr. —— (whom she now calls "Albert" for the first time) made for her.

Shug realizes things have changed. She wants to know what the two of them do together. Celie responds that sewing and idle conversation fill their time together. Shug, who was not born yesterday, wants to know *how* "idle" the conversation is. Celie realizes that she has the upper hand and could play on Shug's scarcely concealed jealousy. In a redemptive moment she elects not to. We talk, she says, about you and how much we love you.

12

LOVE IN THE MIDST OF HORROR
George Dennison, *Luisa Domic*

Samuel Crossman, back in the seventeenth century, wrote a hymn the first stanza of which goes:

My song is love unknown,
My Savior's love to me,
Love to the loveless shown
That they might lovely be.

Faithful to the orthodoxy of his time, Crossman was describing God's love as embodied in the life of Jesus of Nazareth, the special quality of that life being captured with the line, "love to the loveless shown." One effect of that love, Crossman believed, was to instill in its recipients a desire to love others as they themselves had been loved, "that they might lovely be."

In our time, the word "lovely" has become for the most part an ineffective adjective, too overworked to evoke a deep response ("Oh, what a lovely party!") and too weak to communicate with power (a "lovely idea" is one we need not take too seriously). Perhaps only in the hands of an Alan Paton can the word truly be redeemed as we travel with him "a lovely road from Ixopo into the hills" and are led to cry for the beloved country—a journey undertaken in chapter 8, above. And yet there is no other word that quite does justice to George Dennison's haunting novel *Luisa Domic*. It is a genuinely "lovely" creation, both tender and strong, celebrating love in the midst of horror.

It could at first seem incongruous to employ Crossman's lines to describe the impact of *Luisa Domic,* a book in which God is only fleetingly referred to, usually by doubters, and we must not make the connections too tidy. We, and the characters in *Luisa Domic,* live in a more complex world than Crossman's, devoid of the simplicities of faith that he could embrace, and the distance between those worlds must not be minimized. But there is also a virtue in juxtaposing seemingly incongruous things so that they may illumine one another. It was this impulse, for example, that led Albert Camus, early in his writing career, to comment:

> There is beauty and there are the humiliated. Whatever difficulties the enterprise may present, I would like never to be unfaithful either to the one or the other. (*Lyrical and Critical Essays,* pp. 169–170)

Dennison himself poses incongruities that sensitize us not only to horror, with which he acquaints us vividly, but to its polar opposites as well. His book is a hymn to the power of deep love and affection, at the farthest remove from horror. There is love between children in a family; between children and their parents; between a man and a woman, husband and wife; between two men; between friends long separated and then reunited; between strangers who can no longer remain strangers when brought within love's spell; and between all of these people and their joy in the breathtaking beauty of October days and nights in Maine.

The plot line is simple and almost conventional, although what the author does with it is complicated and unconventional: several very different worlds are suddenly juxtaposed. One is the world of the narrator, the father in an extraordinarily loving but quite human family living in Maine. Another is the world of the victim of an extraordinarily unloving and quite demonic regime in Chile, in the days of a bloody coup (a coup engineered, we must acknowledge sadly and angrily, with the active assistance of the United States). Inhabitants of yet another world—the world of creative artistry in New York City—help to mediate the situation when Luisa Domic, a Chilean professional pianist, the only survivor in her family of the atrocities that accompanied Pinochet's takeover, is an unexpected guest of the family in Maine.

What George Dennison manages to communicate in this story is that the tenderness and care and gracious courtesy that exist between people of such diverse backgrounds has the power to stave off, for a few moments, the otherwise unmitigated horror that has become the daily life of Luisa Domic, whose husband and children have been brutally killed in ways that leave her still in a state of shock.

The thread that serves to weave these lives together so tenderly is music.

Two strangers, the man from New York who is a composer, and the woman from Chile who is a performer, uncover, with the help of the others, bonds that make human creativity continue to be possible, as both draw on the power of music, deeper than any words can express, to unite separated and threatened lives.

The gentle pieties do not sustain for long, however. Dennison is a realist and not a sentimentalist, and by the end of the story death and destruction have claimed another victim, Luisa herself. But even out of that defeat, the life of Ida, the young daughter of the book's narrator, is moved in new directions. Apprised of Luisa's self-inflicted death, she does not give way to despair. Within the deepness and darkness of the night, she refuses to succumb to the howling outside; she plays the flute in her room, her musical offering a deed not so much of defiance as of affirmation, a choice to align herself with beauty, frail though it seems to be, rather than horror, strong as it presently appears. And her father, fearful of what the message of death may have done to her, is himself healed as he listens to her act of clear choice. Not one given to prayer (although his life is more of a prayer than he would know or probably want to concede), he can on this occasion, drawing strength from his daughter, form words that go, "Protect her, Lord . . . if You exist . . . if You will."

Luisa Domic can do for a reader what Samuel Crossman wished for the singers of his hymn. It shows us a beguiling loveliness so that, in its presence, we wish that we, too, "might lovely be." It commends to us, as the dictionary tells us loveliness should, "those qualities that inspire love, affection, or admiration." It presents qualities that, as the dictionary further reminds us, are "morally or spiritually attractive."

It does so without any false notes of preachiness or sentimentality. The children not only relate, they fight. The husband and wife are at one point on the edge of a serious quarrel. The narrator and his close friend have a temporary falling out. For so life goes. But behind and beneath and before all that, are affection, caring, and gentle strength. These are the qualities— particularly when set against the monstrous revelations of the Chilean massacre—we would most like to be descriptive of our lives.

Underlying them all is something else: wonder. Wonder at the sheer beauty of the contours of the pastured hills and the spirit-sustaining forests; wonder at the V-formation of the migrating geese; wonder at dolphins and swallows and greyhounds and falcons, who share an ability to make us say "Oh!" with an inflection of gratitude.

There is even a further refinement of wonder. There is, as the author points out, "the 'Oh' of delight, or of admiration touched by love, and the 'Oh' of praise and tribute, of admiration touched by awe." And yet somehow love and awe, even when so carefully distinguished, finally belong together. Which is itself a source of wonder.

The greatest wonder of all is the music. Harold, a composer now using his music as therapy for handicapped children, is able thereby to reach them on deeper levels than words can do. And Harold is likewise able to do that for Luisa, who unexpectedly emits an endless and piercing succession of screams of horror as the recollection of what has so recently happened to her family becomes overpowering. Harold goes to the piano, sits down, and begins to play to her screaming.

> Where we others had been trying to calm her, to bring her back to normal, Harold's piano had gone out to her and found her where she was. Nor was he simply duplicating her voice, but receiving it and enfolding it in a structure that, however minimal, constituted a kind of music that could not be heard in her voice. It was this music, really, that achieved the human presence beside her in what one would have thought would be an absolute darkness of agony. That presence could do nothing, or little, about her agony, or about the outrage of soul, nevertheless it *was* a presence, and it said persistently, *I am with you. I am with you.*

There is indeed a wonder here—that the sound of a piano can "speak" to the sound of a person in the deepest distress, and draw that person gradually from desperation to a moment close to beatitude, and that the resultant evening, after the shattering cry of horror, can become for all a time of sharing, of mutuality, of laughter, of—yes—love.

It is hard, as we look at our world, to avoid a conclusion that sometimes tempts the narrator: "There is no hope. . . . Our world is doomed." And it is a gift to live with Dennison's creation, so that we too can accept what the narrator does with that cry of alarm: "No, no," he finally contradicts himself, humankind is "great and endlessly surprising."

13

FANTASY IN THE MIDST OF "REALITY"
Ursula LeGuin, *Always Coming Home*

Soren Kierkegaard, in a fit of carefully calculated wistfulness, issued a plea at the end of his *Concluding Unscientific Postscript:*

> And, oh, that no half-learned man would lay a dialectical hand upon this work, but would let it stand as it now stands!

Kierkegaard, a master of style and form, chose his modes of literary expression to conform to the subject matter with which he was dealing at the moment. It would have been the supreme insult for a critic (i.e., a "half-learned man") to have commented on his work in such a way as to imply, "Now what Kierkegaard was *really* trying to say, was this . . ."

I cite this caution because I propose to discuss two imaginary literary creations in flat, analytical prose, and the sole point of the prose must be to steer the reader toward the two imaginative literary creations.

The occasion for this exercise is the recent publication of Ursula LeGuin's "novel" (a term open to examination) *Always Coming Home.* In it she has, with marvelous imaginative skill, created a world, a language, a culture, a topography, that merits favorable comparison to J. R. R. Tolkien's trilogy, *The Lord of the Rings.* The two works are in a class by themselves, and (as I will try to show) possess the added virtue of mutually reinforcing one another and enriching our own appreciation of "other worlds" in ways that neither can as fully do alone.

Is *Always Coming Home* a "novel," as its cover proclaims? If so, it is a most unusual novel, but since the unusual is what we have come to expect from its author, we can afford to enlarge our definition. There is, to be sure, a short novel within it, named for its narrator, Stone Telling, presented in three separate sections that total 109 of the 525 pages—barely a fifth of the whole. The story is surrounded by everything under the sun: songs, charts, musings of "Pandora" (to whom we shall return), short stories, poems, romantic tales, creation myths, histories, life stories, dramatic works (including a counterpart of Job, entitled "Chandi," that is extraordinary), geographical information, maps, a portion of another novel. And then there is "The Back of the Book," 116 pages of essays, notes on such topics as musical instruments, medical practices, and making love, concluding with a "Glossary" of Kesh language that is really a miniature dictionary—the only dictionary I have ever read straight through, and which, if a little short on plot, is great on concepts. As if this were not enough, the book has well over a hundred beautiful line drawings by Margaret Chodos, and the case in which the book comes includes a cassette containing music of the Kesh by Todd Barton, along with poems in the original Kesh language. Maybe the $25 price tag isn't so preposterous after all.

On the surface, all of the above sounds like a recipe for disaster. But it is held together by the sheer magic of the author's creative mind—a fact that will occasion no surprise to those who have read any of LeGuin's twenty previous books, which range from science fiction to fantasy, with some poetry, short stories, essays, and historical fiction thrown in. This skill enables her to create her own kind of suspense in *Always Coming Home*. It is not the suspense we experience in a "straight" novel, where we are always wondering what will come next in the plot line, but rather the suspense of constantly wondering what piece of the puzzle this new section—whether song, poem, drama, or map—will put in place. Only gradually does it all come together, and we stay with it until the end, not only because we want to know how it *does* come together, but also because initially odd names gradually become old friends that we recognize: "heyimas," for example, or "wakwa," even though references to the "hinge" remain appropriately tantalizing. We have become part of the story.

It is possible, of course, that a prospective reader won't get hooked. (Some people are not even hooked by Tolkien.) Their loss. But I predict that those who enter, even tentatively, into the valley of the Kesh will hang in there, intrigued, challenged, and finally captivated.

Archaeology of the Future

How does one enter the land of the Kesh? If this were archaeology of the past, the technique would be clear: "digs," classification of shards and other relics of

ancient civilization, painstaking accumulation of evidence, all rationally
ordered. But this is "archaeology of the future," an anthropological report on
a world that does not yet exist, save in Ursula LeGuin's mind. Imagination,
not research, is the key to entrance, and she tells us wonderfully how to find it:

> You take your child or grandchild in your arms, a young baby, not yet a year old,
> and go down into the wild oats in the field below the barn. Stand quietly.
> Perhaps the baby will see something or hear a voice, or speak to somebody
> there, somebody from home. (p. 5)

Those lacking the requisite child or grandchild can still, thanks to the
author, enter the world of the Kesh people, who are living at a point far distant
in the future in northern California, after some massive geological upheavals
and rearrangements. (As one who lives within two miles of the ever-
threatening San Andreas Fault, I have a vested interest in this information.)
The setting is not, as some critics mistakenly supposed, the world after a
nuclear holocaust. The author feels that it would be immoral to put a story in
such a setting, since it might lend credence to the notion that living beings
could survive a nuclear war.

Even without nuclear war, however, there has been a lot of human
destruction by toxic waste and befouling of the atmosphere, and the situation
has reverted to a kind of primitive culture with few of the so-called "amenities
of civilization." One survival has been a sophisticated computer system that
seemed initially out of place to me, representing one of the few anomalies I
found in the cultural world of *Always Coming Home*. But I later discovered (in
correspondence with the author) that I had missed the point. What is
"sophisticated" is not so much the computer system as the carefully limited use
made of it by the people. One is forced to realize that this presumably
"primitive" culture is really more advanced than our own; it is wise enough to
use technological competence to construct washing machines but not Trident
missiles and is content with a wood-burning steam train rather than an
airplane that can get from Washington to Tokyo in two hours. Technology
remains a servant rather than a master.

The theme of the novel, a familiar one to LeGuin readers, is clearly tele-
graphed by the title *Always Coming Home*. Stone Telling's story, imbedded
within the book, is a quintessential quest story, involving a valley woman who,
because her father is a Condor from outside the valley, feels alienated from her
surroundings and leaves home to accompany him to the land of the warlike
Condors, where she feels even more alienated. Escaping at considerable peril,
she returns to the people and valley of Kesh, where she settles back in with a
newfound self-understanding resulting from her journey. She has discovered

that "home" is both the place she had gone out from, and the place to which she has returned. She is, throughout the journey, "always coming home."

In many of Ursula LeGuin's novels the same theme is central. Ged, the mage in *A Wizard of Earthsea,* oversteps the bounds of his craft and has to take a long journey to discover his true self in a hazardous encounter, after which, but only after which, he, too, can return home. Genly Ai, in *The Left Hand of Darkness,* makes a similar pilgrimage, this time to another planet, before he can return home knowing himself in a way he did not know himself before. Shevek goes on another such pilgrimage in *The Dispossessed.* Such journeys provide extended commentary on T. S. Eliot's lines in the concluding portion of *Little Gidding:*

> We shall not cease from exploration
> And the end of all our exploring
> Will be to arrive where we started
> And know the place for the first time.

It is the willingness to venture elsewhere that enables us to return to the place of departure and know not only "the place," (as Eliot says), but ourselves (as LeGuin adds) "for the first time."

Two Quests

It is LeGuin's use of the quest story that provides a point for comparison with Tolkien's *The Lord of the Rings,* previously noted. The two authors have created not only worlds of incredible intricacy and detail, but both of those worlds are the scene of quest stories. In LeGuin, as we have seen, the images are circular or cyclical. A protagonist starts out, goes somewhere, and finally returns to the place of departure. But the quest story can also be told with linear imagery, as Tolkien and others have demonstrated; the quest begins at Point A and (after many marvelous adventures) ends at Point B, or more likely Point F or Point L. The fulfillment of the quest comes elsewhere than at the point of departure: the princess is rescued from the dungeon deep in enemy territory, the treasure is found in a distant land, Christian finally makes it to the Celestial City, or (as in the case of Tolkien's Frodo Baggins) the evil ring is deposited in the far-distant Mount Doom and the evil powers are thereby thwarted.

But the two forms of the quest story are not quite that distinct. There is a cyclical thrust, for example, in Tolkien's earlier story, *The Hobbit,* with its revealing subtitle, *There and Back Again.* In that adventure, Bilbo Baggins's quest is not ended when he finally arrives at the far-off lair of Smaug and recovers the treasure. The return journey is in some ways fraught with even greater peril, since greed for the treasure infects members of the questing band and shatters the unity of purpose they had had at the beginning.

The theme of "return" is also helpful in reassessing Frodo's quest in *The Lord of the Rings*. His goal is clear; deposit the ring in Mount Doom and thus insure that its power is annulled. The goal (which occupies most of the three volumes) is finally achieved after great hardship. The story does not end there, although in relation to the work as a whole the return journey initially seems more like a coda than a climax. But Frodo has been deeply scarred by his journey, so there is diminution as well as gain. During his absence, the Shire has been taken over by remnants of the evil forces whose ultimate defeat his quest had ensured. And so, although the campaign has been won, mopping up operations must continue and the Shire must be "scoured," before Frodo's journey is complete. In this sense, his final point of arrival is identical with his initial point of departure, and we seem to have a parallel to the quest of Stone Telling, whose return to the valley gradually brings a sense of completion to her life. She has been "always coming home."

That is surely what Frodo desires, but it is not what he receives. Although Sam, his faithful companion, is able to fit back in, Frodo has been so changed between his departure and return that peace and contentment in the Shire cannot be his lot. He has been "too deeply hurt," as he tells Sam. Sometimes, he continues, when things are in danger, "someone has to give them up, lose them, so that others might keep them," and they are denied enjoyment of the fruits of their perilous labors. (One is reminded of Moses, leading his people to the very portals of the Promised Land and being denied entry himself.)

Tolkien's resolution of the unfairness of this outcome can only be achieved eschatologically, a solution that is not proposed in Ursula LeGuin's novel. There *is* redemption for Frodo, but it is a redemption beyond the confines of the Shire and of Middle Earth itself, and Tolkien beautifully describes Frodo's journey from the Grey Havens across the sea to the far west, where he beholds "white shores and beyond them a far green country under a swift sunrise." Only there is the quest finished.

So the cyclical pattern is finally inadequate for Tolkien's purposes, and a linear pattern reasserts itself as the guarantor of the coherence and fulfillment of the quest.

History and Nature

In these diverse understandings of quest we can see a basic difference between the two authors. Oversimplifying to make the point, we can observe that the interpretative principle for Tolkien and his linear pattern is *history,* while the interpretative principle for LeGuin and her cyclical pattern is *nature.*

To be sure, there is lavish attention to nature in Tolkien; he has, after all, created a whole cosmos. In it, the seasons play a significant role; nature can be both protagonist and antagonist, the flora and fauna make a difference to the questers, the magical snowstorm makes Mount Caradras impassable, and so on. But the main thrust is surely linear; the progression is from the Shire to Rivendell to Lothlorien to Minas Tirath to Minas Morgul, and then across Gorgoroth to Mount Doom. It is finally the will and determination and choices of the hobbits, rather than the landscape or the cycle of seasons, that determine the outcome.

Similarly, while there is a share of that in *Always Coming Home,* particularly in the experiences of Stone Telling, the activities of the inhabitants of the valley are preponderantly responses to, and relationships with, nature rather than history. Centrality is given to the dances that mark the various seasons of the year. There is a lyric acceptance of lessons to be learned from the water, the planting of crops, the message of the fog. The relationship with nature is so deep and significant as to be reciprocal: "It was a long way I went before a spring let me find it," Stone Telling reports (p. 20). Nature, rather than human nature, provides the gentle and sustaining images: seeing cattle, one is reminded that "The sound of their cowbells / is like the ringing of water" (p. 70). Musicians, rather than being described by their effect on persons, "make flutes of the rivers, make drums of the hills." Stone Telling's story, the author acknowledges, is "as near to history as we have come."

Furthermore, in contrast to Tolkien's virtually sexless world, in which procreation would seem possible only by parthenogenesis, LeGuin's world, with its emphases on nature, not only does not avoid but glories in fecundity, reproduction, procreation, and rituals of sexual arousal, in which sex is not only good in itself but replicates on the human level the mystery of ongoingness in the natural order.

Fortunately, we are not called to choose between these two visions, for we cannot live in one to the exclusion of the other. It is the inevitability of our immersion in both realms that is both the glory and the pain of the human venture—one of the most enduring theological insights, it might be added, of Reinhold Niebuhr. Neither LeGuin nor Tolkien force an either/or choice on us. They simply create their amalgams of history and nature with different priorities and proportions. If we need more of the historical dimension than LeGuin provides, we also need more of the rootedness in the natural order than Tolkien provides. Much as we need Tolkien's stress on history in times of human peril like our own, we need equally the ability to measure the meaning of our lives by more than the morning headlines, and LeGuin refreshingly opens up entire dimensions we might otherwise neglect, to our peril. As we measure our own world against other worlds, whether Kesh or Middle Earth, we need both visions.

Fantasy's Gifts to Us

But how do we engage in such measuring? Put more crassly, what is the utility of works of fantasy such as these?

It is presently fashionable to dismiss fantasy as "escapist," a morally delinquent device by which we remove ourselves from the pressures of the "real world" that so often immobilize us into uncaring. Tolkien has a rejoinder to this charge: It all depends, he says, on that from which one is escaping. "Why," he asks in his essay "On Fairy Tales," "should a man be scorned if, finding himself in prison, he tries to get out and go home?" There is all the difference in the world, Tolkien reminds us, between the escape of the prisoner and the flight of the deserter.

One way by which we can be motivated to "escape" from an undesirable situation is to discover an alternative set of possibilities and seek to introduce them into our situation. Alternative models make it possible to entertain the possibility of change. When there is no vision, it has been remarked, the people perish, and the hallmark of fantasy is to provide new models and thereby new visions. And here is Ursula LeGuin's greatest gift to us. As we enter into the lives of the Kesh people, for example, we find much that offers alternatives to our situation. I have already noted the modest use that is made of advanced technological expertise, and how the restraint thus exercised is beneficent rather than destructive. Technology, as the author has pointed out, is ever with us, even when we do such rudimentary things as setting pen to paper or cooking a meal. So she creates a people who have made a conscious decision to settle for a nonindustrial technology, even when the blandishments of "hi-tech" could be easily retrieved. And since it is hi-tech that dominates our own lives, with increasingly destructive consequences, we need the challenge of a fantasy that strips hi-tech of its demonic attraction and offers a radically different technology in its stead.

Another illustration: Almost in passing, the author offers an alternative view of ownership and wealth. "The Kesh grammar," she comments, "makes no provision for a relationship of ownership between living things. [Kesh is] a language in which . . . 'to be rich' is the same word as 'to give' " (p. 42, cf. p. 510). Later: "Wealth consists not in *things* but in an *act*; the act of giving" (p. 112). The same noun in Kesh can be translated into English as "wealth" and as "generosity." "In such terms," she remarks, "people who don't own much because they keep giving things away are rich, while those who give little and so own much are poor" (p. 128). The Condors are criticized because "Their wealth did not flow; they did not give with pleasure" (p. 195). In this slender theme, cropping up here and there, we have not only an indictment of our own culture but also a recipe for transformation.

The theme is important enough to illustrate by reference to an earlier book of LeGuin's, *The Left Hand of Darkness*. On the planet Gethen, the relation of the sexes is very different from sexual relations on the planet Earth. Gethenians have both male and female sexual organs and they never know ahead of time which will be activated during the frequent mating seasons (Kemmer). Thus a given individual may, during the course of a lifetime, be both a mother and a father, and for many periods of time will be neither an active male or female, but simply a person. (The arrangement makes it possible during the course of the novel to report that "The King is pregnant.")

In commenting on this highly unusual arrangement, Robert Scholes suggests that "such a deliberate variation on human sexuality can help us to see the realities of our own sexual situation more clearly, and to feel them more deeply." On the planet Earth the major responsibility for child rearing inevitably falls upon the women, and the male is relatively free during the childbearing years. But on Gethen, no single person is likely to be as "tied down" as a woman elsewhere, nor to be as free from responsibility as men are elsewhere.

And while men and women on planet Earth cannot create a sexual arrangement like that on Gethen, they can, once apprised of the Gethen arrangement, so restructure their own lives that there is more equality and sharing in the raising of children than has usually been part of a heterosexual society. One can leave the fantasy world and return to the "real" world to live life in a transformed way.

"Pandora" as Guide

Such considerations sharpen the question of how we make connections between the vision in a book and the assumptions we bring to a book. How is creative interplay possible between the book and the reader? The problem exists for authors as well as readers, and scattered through *Always Coming Home* are a series of reflections by "Pandora," whom we gradually come to realize is the author herself, struggling to be a responsible, rather than a manipulative, transmitter of the Kesh culture to the rest of us. It will be rewarding to trace her journey in establishing such connections.

Pandora's initial comments indicate perplexity at the nature of the task of relating book and reader. She "worries about what she is doing" (p. 53). Her decision finally is to share "bits, chunks, fragments," and "let the heart complete the pattern." There will be no hard sell; only a sharing. A good start.

Her second entry draws us into the valley a little more; it is simply the description of a creek at the time of the summer dancing (p. 95). By the third entry, however, her "worry" has escalated to "agitation" and some designedly disjointed reflections. Pandora has opened the box, and like her mythic forebear, a lot of evils have come forth and she is necessarily in collusion with their spread. ("Am I not a citizen of the State that fought the first nuclear war?") She hopes that under everything else in the book, "underneath the war, plague, famine, holocaust," there will be hope. Even if the box is empty, examining it provides some room and some time to look forward and backward. But the agitation remains (pp. 147–148).

Pandora experiences a breakthrough, however, in the fourth meditation (pp. 239–241). Still "worrying," she nevertheless finds "a way into the valley," a mode of transition from her world (and ours) into the world of the Kesh, so that she is no longer an intruder but an inhabitant. The key that unlocks the door is nature, not history. It is a meditation on the scrub oak that puts her in tune for the first time with the new world of her own creation, and it is significant that from here on Pandora no longer describes herself as "worrying."

Her next appearance betokens the change of mood. She is not only more relaxed, but even feisty, as she converses aggressively with one of her characters, the archivist at a library in the valley ("I never did like smartass utopians"). Nor does she like the archivist's description of what Pandora is doing ("An Up Yours to the people who ride snowmobiles, make nuclear weapons and run prison camps, by a middle-aged housewife"). Even so, or perhaps because of the honesty, the conversation ends with the archivist and Pandora singing together. The empathy is deepening.

The next time around Pandora, by now a significant participant with the people of the valley, "gently" offers to widen that participation to include the reader (p. 339). Thus far her descriptions have drawn the reader along, and the reader assumes at each point on the journey that they have arrived ("Let's stop here, this is it!"). But it isn't, and the response must be, "a little farther yet." After a rest, the journey must continue, but now in reciprocal relationship: "We have a long way yet to go, and I can't go without you." The author pays her readers the extreme tribute of acknowledging that she needs them just as much as they need her, and that increasing participation is the price—and the reward—for continuing.

Pandora's identification with the valley is complete enough so that in "The Back of the Book" (pp. 486–487), she can burst into poetry, forsaking

"The City of Man" (the closest remnant of her own civilization) and opting to live with the natives of the Valley, "away from the Kingdom," content to "live with the animals and plants, / eating and praising them / and die with them." Turning her back on "Newton" and all that a scientifically ordered world implies, she will trust "wind, the rainbow, / mist, still air."

Lest this suggest that nature has totally engulfed history and neglected humanity, Pandora's final entry is gloriously entitled "Pandora No Longer Worrying" (pp. 506–507). In it she "takes hands and dances with her friends." The passage is her expression of thanksgiving to the many people who helped her write the book. If nature has been the warp of her creative loom, people are still the woof. The worlds have come together; not only the worlds of nature and history, but the worlds of Kesh and contemporaneity. (A sign: the singers on the tape provided with the book have had Kesh names added to their contemporary names.) To be rid of worry, we learn from Pandora, is to be empowered to acts of gratitude.

This is a remarkable conclusion to a remarkable journey, illustrating the gradual movement from the sheer juxtaposition of two incommensurate worlds to a situation in which the strange "other" world has not only been entered, but can provide new perceptions of our own world. We are invited to a dual citizenship, not unlike the dual citizenship accorded the musicians. As a result of the change in the backdrop of human activity, human activity itself is transformed. The movement from worry to gratitude is as vast a movement as we are capable of making.

Ursula LeGuin faults one of her novels, *The Word for World Is Forest*, by saying that she "succumbed, in part, to the lure of the pulpit." The book, set in the distant future on another planet, was occasioned by, and spoke to, the struggle of the Vietnam years. Pulpit or not, LeGuin, and all the writers we have encountered in the above pages, proclaim. They want their works to make a difference in the lives of their readers, and, whether directly or not, they are challenging their readers to change. A fantasy like *Always Coming Home* will teach, even if not directly. It will not only force us to make judgments about the fantasy world and its inhabitants, but in doing so it will also provide a mirror in which to see our own world and those who live in it. If we do not like what we see in the mirror, fantasy can invite us to reexplore who we are and what things count for us, in order to reestablish all that is highest and deepest and truest in us and in our world. Like all art, fantasy can—and let W. H. Auden and Ursula LeGuin have the last and best word—"persuade us to rejoice" and teach us "how to praise."

EPILOGUE
Persuaded to Rejoice

[The purpose of art] is to persuade us to rejoice and teach us how to praise.

—Ursula LeGuin's summary of Auden's theme in "The Crab Nebula, the Paramecium and Tolstoy"

If we refer again to the words of Auden in the epigraph of this volume, we will discover that he proposes a second admonition for the poet, to which we have so far paid scant attention. Not only is the poet to "persuade us to rejoice," but also to teach us "how to praise." It is my conviction that for Auden, and for Ursula LeGuin as well, this is not so much a new admonition as a second way of enforcing the initial concern by the stylistic device of "parallelism" (a device also found in many of the psalms), in which a single theme is repeated a second time with different words so the reader cannot escape its importance.

As with Auden's admonition to "rejoice," the admonition to "praise" is realistically rather than sentimentally situated. Out of hitherto unproductive and hostile land, a vineyard is to be raised by the poet's verses. "Unsuccess" and "distress" are to be subjects of singing and even rapture; there is, once again, to be celebration. Resources for this seemingly impossible task must come from within. Surprisingly, it is "in the deserts of the heart" that the poet must "let the healing fountain start"—"deserts" and "fountains" being a most unlikely but necessary juxtaposition. And thus nurtured, prison (whether real, or simply a metaphor for human existence) becomes the place where it is truly possible to "teach the free man how to praise," "prison" and "freedom" being an equally unlikely but necessary juxtaposition.

Building on this, we may note that to "praise" something is to "prize" it, to find value in it, to make it worth our acclaim. As with rejoicing, praising is an expression of gratitude, by means of which we commend to others the value of something and give it our stamp of approval. Like rejoicing, praising is a communal act, but even more so. We may gather the folks to "rejoice" (as the shepherd and the widow did way back in the Introduction) but when we "praise" we are likely to ask others to join in a toast or a song or a refrain or even a prayer of adulation, as we commend to each other the value of the one to whom we offer praise.

It makes a difference to whom we offer praise. If we have been moved by a *book,* for example, we praise the author by writing a favorable review or buying copies for our friends (a splendid way to show praise, as any author will attest), or by reading portions of the book aloud to others. If we have been helped by another *person,* we commend that person to others as worthy of esteem, perhaps by a recital of good deeds done or confidences honored, and thereby seek to widen the circle of human relationships. If we keep our eyes open, we may be moved to praise the entire *universe,* or at least (with Immanuel Kant) "the starry heavens above and the moral law beneath," glad for a place within which praise and rejoicing are possible. If we are religious, we will recognize that the highest praise is accorded to *God,* and will join the whole creation (including "whales and all that move in the waters," as the ancient canticle of praise, *Benedicite, omnia opera Domini,* reminds us) in acknowledging the divine beneficence under which we receive such gifts as books and persons, whales and dolphins. The worst thing, as a student of mine once told me, drawing on Schleiermacher without knowing it, would be to discover that there was no one to whom praise could be offered, or thanks rendered, especially in those fleeting moments when scepticism has been washed away by the tides of gratitude.

All very well . . . for our high moments. But what about the low moments—the moments when books fail us, persons betray us, the universe is cruel, God is absent or powerless or malevolent, and whatever gratitude we once had has been washed away by new tides of scepticism? How, then, can someone "persuade us to rejoice," or teach us "how to praise"?

Acknowledging that there are no tidy "answers" to such questions and that there is no faith so pure as to offer guarantees against future struggles with despair, it may still be worth a quick, retrospective glance over the authors to whom we have listened in these pages, to see if their cumulative wisdom can help us tilt, at least now and then, toward rejoicing and praising, rather than toward lamenting and debunking. No one can truly take this journey for another, and my own attempt will be no more than an invitation to others to undertake a similar exploration.

The authors and books we have encountered can help "persuade us to rejoice" in a variety of ways—some by affirming on their own authority things we hoped, but could not believe on our own authority, were true; others by dispelling illusions that were making our vision murky; and a few by confronting us with options that may never have occurred to us.

We can rejoice, for example, that communication is possible through the printed page, since it means that even when we seem to be solitary, we are not alone but are part of a large, if invisible, community, examining common perplexities that would overwhelm us if we were solely "on our own." There is no promise of unanimity in that community, but there is an invitation and a promise to hear one another out and take one another seriously, whether we are playwrights or archbishops, Tennessee Williams or William Temple. (Chapter 2.)

We can rejoice whenever authors share perplexities as well as assurances, even though the perplexities may be more initially compelling than the assurances. Since we are all vulnerable, it helps to discover that we are not alone in our vulnerability, and that together we can usually shed more light on the darkness than any one of us can do alone. (Chapter 2.)

We can rejoice when people of differing convictions disavow cheap shots, and seek, as far as possible, to practice empathy toward one another—Dante entering imaginatively into the circle of hell, a world without grace, and tasting its compelling power so that he will not be tempted to offer frivolous alternatives to it, and Albert Camus giving the Christian option an agonizingly fair hearing in ways that make his final refusal poignant, and (perhaps for that reason) not quite final. (Chapters 2 and 7.)

We can rejoice when dissimilar vocabularies point in similar directions, and vice versa, each illuminating the blind spots of the other, each challenging and being challenged, each acknowledging that no words can fully penetrate the mystery of why we are here and what we are supposed to do about it, so that Ignazio Silone looks for a new vocabulary in order to be honest, and Charles Williams seeks to invest our ordinary words with extraordinary new dimensions of meaning. (Chapters 2, 4, and 6.)

We can rejoice that when confronted by evil there are always a few (like Nathan) who, rather than being seduced into its service, elect to stand against it, thereby empowering us to do the same. (Chapter 1.)

We can rejoice when a story, worlds removed from ours (so we had supposed) turns out to be a shattering yet ultimately healing recapitulation of our own story (as David had to learn the hard way). We can rejoice, similarly, when kings are held accountable for lapses from accountability, and take heart when common, ordinary folk occasionally rise to heights of moral greatness. (Chapter 1.)

We can rejoice that even when we wait in fear and unknowing (as do Beckett's tramps), simply staying the course when there is no earthly reason to do so, we get glimpses of a resiliency in the human spirit toward which we can also aspire. (Chapter 3.)

We can rejoice that when everything crumbles, when hopes are dashed, when "law and order" work against us, when admission to the "castle" of our human hopes is denied us (as it was denied to Kafka's character Joseph K), even then there is a fleeting wisp of hope: that to which we are not entitled may nevertheless be granted us gratuitously. (Chapter 3.)

We can rejoice that every now and then an old story (about angels' songs and wise men's gifts) that seemed devoid of power to persuade is restored to us in a new idiom that makes its reception entertainable, with broad hints that for us, too, "the time being" can be "redeemed from insignificance." (Chapter 3.)

We can rejoice that some stories are worth telling and retelling, generation after generation (as Ignazio Silone discovered), and that they can energize not only a refusal to surrender to evil but a belief that maintaining one's integrity is worth the pain. (Chapter 4.)

We can rejoice that names for "God," manipulated by evil people for unjust ends, can (as Silone also discovered) be erased, and new names for God chalked on the slate of human history—names that are given substance by simple folk whose deeds redefine the human spirit and provide clues for a new understanding of the divine spirit. (Chapter 4.)

We can *never* rejoice in the existence of death camps. But we *can* rejoice that in the darkest corners of the kingdom of night, minute flashes of light illumine human beings (like Elie Wiesel) who refuse to surrender their humanity, who refuse to be complicit in the evil that surrounds them, and who, with every reason to deny God, refuse to do that as well. They wait, not as Beckett's tramps or Auden's shepherds wait, but as those who, since a promise was given, refuse against all odds to relinquish final trust in the Promise-Giver. (Chapter 5.)

We can rejoice that when people no longer have answers, they still persist (again like Elie Wiesel, and Camus's Jean-Baptiste Clamence, and C. S. Lewis's Orual and a host of others) in asking questions, and that their willingness to persevere in a world that denies them answers witnesses again to the toughness of the human spirit. (Chapters 5, 7, and 9.)

We can rejoice that images drawn from the human experience we know so well are helpful pointers (as Charles Williams demonstrated) toward that which transcends our experience—suggesting that the commonplace is truly the dwelling place of the holy. (Chapters 6 and 9.)

We can rejoice that creators of the most searing descriptions of the human situation, unyielding in the pessimism of their portraiture and despairingly honest in their descriptions of human folly, nevertheless resist going the full road of negation (even an Albert Camus), and leave apertures, however tiny, through which might someday be heard not only the predictable laughter of judgment, but likewise the unpredictable laughter of joy. (Chapter 7.)

We can rejoice in the integrity of writers (like Alan Paton) who refuse to offer easy "religious" answers, and who are willing to display the vulnerability of their faith and the ways it can be used for both good and evil. (Chapter 8.)

We can rejoice that when everything has caved in, there is still a voice that refuses to be silenced (like that of the police captain) reminding us that the last word must continue to be restoration rather than destruction. (Chapter 8.)

We can rejoice (with Paton's Tante Sophie) that even when the gravest of offenses have been committed, we must find ways to use them so virtue can be reborn. (Chapter 8.)

We can rejoice at the willingness of people to continue their age-old complaints against the gods (as Orual does), demanding answers, and then revising their complaints in the light of new insights and complexities. (Chapter 9.)

We can rejoice that attempts to live life solely on our own terms are overridden (as Buechner's Brendan discovered). When aspirants for sainthood falsely seek God far away in order to avoid confronting God near at hand, the rest of us can get the message: attention to those in need is the only way to meet our own needs. (Chapter 10.)

We can rejoice when every now and then our plaintive cries for clarity are denied (as Brendan and Orual found out), and we discover that "seeing through a glass darkly" is not only all we are entitled to but turns out to be more than enough. (Chapters 9 and 10.)

We can rejoice that in situations of deprivation, greatness of character can still be forged, and that (as Alice Walker's Celie discovered) unwillingness to inflict pain signals the beginning of new strength and fresh understanding of God. (Chapter 11.)

We can rejoice that in the midst of all that threatens us, wonder (as Walker and Dennison remind us) enters in when we least expect it and provides us with moments, however small, of healing. (Chapters 11 and 12.)

We can rejoice that not even terror is always and irremediably terror, and that with it (as Luisa Domic found in the midst of strangers who turned out to be friends) tender shoots of love can—at least for a moment—take root, as human beings rally around one another to deal with visions of horror that can neither be fully faced nor be fully effaced. (Chapter 12.)

We can rejoice that differing ways of ordering human life can (as Ursula LeGuin demonstrates) challenge us to critique long-accepted patterns, granting us enough empathy with a new society so that we can never fit back comfortably into the old. (Chapter 13.)

We can rejoice, finally, that we are always part of two stories—our own immediate story and whatever other story the author invites us to enter.

For it is in the tension between two stories that the breakthroughs come.

The final word is a reminder that wholeness (what is elsewhere called "salvation") does not come through words, and that while books can sometimes conduct us to a new threshold, they cannot take us across that threshold. The decisive step can only be taken by ourselves in a deliberately chosen, risk-filled action that later we will recognize as the work of grace. Such a step, if we finally take it, will be repeated frequently in the course of a lifetime—a series of acts of faith sufficiently grounded in love to bequeath us hope—in sequences and arrangements we can never predict ahead of time.

Perhaps the only clue that we are even getting close will be to look around us one day or another, discover that we are in a new place we somehow already recognize, and, in an act that combines "rejoicing" and "praise," be able to lift up our arms, spread them wide, and say exultantly with Tolkien's Niggle, "It's a gift!"

NOTES

In my own text I have used inclusive language. When quoting from other authors I have reproduced their texts as originally written.

Introduction—"Persuade Us to Rejoice"

The Tolkien quotation is from *Tree and Leaf* (Boston: Houghton Mifflin Co., 1965), p. 104. I have dealt more fully with the theme of "liberation" in *Gustavo Gutiérrez: An Introduction to Liberation Theology* (Maryknoll, N.Y., Orbis Books, 1990).

Chapter 1—The Power of a Story: The Nathan Syndrome

Originally published as "The Nathan Syndrome: Stories with a Moral Intention," in *Religion and Literature,* Notre Dame, Ind.: University of Notre Dame (Winter 1984). The middle section dealing with the biblical passage is also found in *Unexpected News: Reading the Bible with Third World Eyes* (Philadelphia: Westminster Press, 1984).

Chapter 2—Cut Flowers, Selective Gratitude, and Assyrians in Modern Dress

Much of this material is new, and the rest has been extensively reworked from "Assyrians in Modern Dress" in *Presbyterian Life* (May, 1962); a chapter on the same theme in *The Pseudonyms of God* (Philadelphia: Westminster Press, 1972), pp. 96–103; and "The Minister and Contemporary Literature," in *Union Theological Seminary Quarterly Review.* I have reflected further on these themes in "My Story and 'The Story'," *Theology Today* (July, 1975).

Chapter 3—Four Ways of Waiting: A Case Study

Originally published as "The Theme of Waiting in Modern Literature," in *Ramparts* (Summer 1964). The quotations from Tillich at the beginning and end of the chapter are in *The Shaking of the Foundations* (London: SCM Press, 1949), pp. 151 and 152. The Salinger quotations are from *Franny and Zooey* (Boston: Little, Brown & Co., 1961), pp. 7–8. The Beckett material is from *Waiting for Godot, A Tragicomedy in Two Acts* (New York: Grove Press, 1954), passim. The Kafka material is from Kafka, *The Trial* (New York: Alfred A. Knopf, 1937), and *The Castle* (New York: Alfred A. Knopf, 1941).

The Camus quotations on Kafka are in Camus, *The Myth of Sisyphus* (London: Hamilton, 1955), pp. 104, 107. Max Brod's "resolution" of the unfinished manuscript of *The Castle* is included in the first edition of the latter work. The Auden material is from "For the Time Being," in *The Collected Poems of W. H. Auden* (New York: Random House, 1945), pp. 405–466. The extended quotations appear *seriatim* in the text.

Chapter 4—Strange Names for a Shapeless God:
Ignazio Silone

Originally published as "Ignazio Silone and the Pseudonyms of God," in Mooney and Staley, eds., *The Shapeless God: Essays on Modern Fiction* (Pittsburgh: University of Pittsburgh Press, 1968), pp. 19–40. I have reflected further on Silone in *The Pseudonyms of God* (Philadelphia: Westminster Press, 1972), Part II. Quotations are from Ignazio Silone, *Bread and Wine,* trans. Eric Mosbacher (New York: New American Library, Signet Classic, 1986), and Ignazio Silone, *Fontamara,* trans. Eric Mosbacher (New York: New American Library, Signet Classic, 1986). English translations for both works are copyright © 1986 Darina Silone. The following notes are citations from the text:

1. In Richard Crossman, ed., *The God That Failed* (New York: Harper & Row, 1949), p. 83.
2. Ibid., p. 86.
3. Ibid., p. 85, italics added. Silone later told the priest that if the devil marionette ever asked where the priest was, he would cheerfully give him the priest's address.
4. Ibid., pp. 113–114.
5. Silone, *Bread and Wine* (New York: New American Library, Signet Classic, 1986), p. 218.
6. Silone, *Fontamara* (New York: New American Library, Signet Classic, 1986), p. 165.
7. Ibid., p. 29.
8. Silone, *Bread and Wine,* p. 17.
9. Silone, *Bread and Wine.* The theme also pervades *The Seed Beneath the Snow.*
10. Silone, *Bread and Wine,* p. 224. The latter theme is developed more fully in Silone's stage version of *Bread and Wine,* entitled *And He Did Hide Himself,* the biblical reference being John 12:36: "These things spake Jesus, and departed, *and [he] did hide himself* from them" (KJV).
11. Ibid., pp. 225.
12. See Isa. 10:5–19.
13. See most recently in Tillich, *Systematic Theology,* III (Chicago: University of Chicago Press, 1963), esp. pp. 152–154.
14. Blaise Pascal, *Pensées,* many editions, nos. 194, 242. The biblical reference is to Isa. 45:15.
15. Silone, *Bread and Wine,* p. 249.
16. Silone, *Fontamara,* p. 155.

17. Silone, *A Handful of Blackberries* (London: Jonathan Cape, Ltd., 1954).
18. Silone, *Bread and Wine*, pp. 117–118.
19. Silone, *The Seed Beneath the Snow*. The same point can be made linguistically from the Latin, *cum-panis*, meaning "with bread," the word from which "companion" is derived. Companions are literally those who share bread together.
20. Silone, *And He Did Hide Himself* (London: Jonathan Cape, 1946), p. 6.
21. Recall the earlier treatment of this theme in *Bread and Wine*.
22. Silone, *The Seed Beneath the Snow*.
23. Pascal, *Pensées*, no. 552, "The Mystery of Jesus."
24. Silone, *Bread and Wine*, p. 264.
25. Ibid., p. 265. The theme is present in the second-century document the *Didache* and is incorporated in most subsequent liturgies.

Chapter 5—The Human Obligation to Question God:
Elie Wiesel

Originally published as "Elie Wiesel: Writer as Peacemaker," in *Christian Century* (November 5, 1986) and reprinted in part in my *Elie Wiesel: Messenger to All Humanity*, 2d ed. (Notre Dame, Ind.: University of Notre Dame Press, 1979), pp. 253–254; "Elie Wiesel's Song," in *Commonweal* (July 12, 1974), portions also in Brown, *Elie Wiesel: Messenger to All Humanity*, pp. 145–147, 157–159; and "*Twilight*: Madness, Caprice, Friendship and God," in Carol Rittner, ed., *Elie Wiesel: Between Memory and Hope* (New York: New York University Press, 1990), pp. 177–187.

The quotations from *Ani Maamin* are found in Wiesel, *Ani Maamin: A Song Lost and Found Again* (New York: Random House, 1973), and are taken *seriatim* from the text. The Buber quotation is from *Israel and the World* (New York: Schocken Books, 1948), pp. 39–40.

The quotations from *Twilight* (New York: Summit Books, 1987), are cited in the text. The Kierkegaard quotation in the last section is from *Either/Or*, Vol. I (Princeton, N.J.: Princeton University Press, 1946), p. 135.

Chapter 6—The Affirmation and Negation of Images:
Charles Williams

Originally published in a much longer version as "Charles Williams: Lay Theologian," *Theology Today* (July, 1953), pp. 212–229. The following are citations from the text:

1. C. S. Lewis, ed., *Essays Presented to Charles Williams* (Oxford: Oxford University Press, 1947), p. ix.
2. C. S. Lewis, *A Preface to Paradise Lost* (Oxford: Oxford University Press, 1949), p. v.
3. In Lewis, ed., *Essays*, p. xiv.
4. Ibid., p. xiv.
5. Williams, *He Came Down from Heaven* (London: Faber & Faber, 1940), p. 30.
6. Lewis, *Essays*, p. xiii.
7. Lewis, *The Arthurian Torso* (Oxford: Oxford University Press, 1948), pp. 142–143.

8. Williams, *The Descent of the Dove* (London: Faber & Faber, 1939), p. 46.
9. Williams, *He Came Down from Heaven*, p. 89.
10. Williams, *The Figure of Beatrice* (London: Faber & Faber, 1943), p. 9.
11. Williams, *He Came Down from Heaven*, p. 72.
12. Williams, *The Figure of Beatrice*, p. 22.
13. Williams, *He Came Down from Heaven*, p. 66.
14. Daniel Jenkins, *The Gift of Ministry* (London: Faber & Faber, 1950), p. 140.
15. See Williams, *The Descent of the Dove*, p. 57.
16. Williams, *The Figure of Beatrice*, pp. 8–10.
17. The source of the phrase, which he once mistakenly attributed to Augustine, was unknown to Williams.
18. Williams, *War in Heaven* (London: Faber & Faber, 1930), p. 137.
19. Williams, *The Descent of the Dove*, p. 181.
20. Williams, *All Hallows' Eve* (London: Faber & Faber, 1945), p. 144.
21. Williams, *War in Heaven*, p. 66.
22. Lewis, *The Arthurian Torso*, p. 105.
23. Williams, *The Descent of the Dove*, p. 15.
24. Williams, *He Came Down from Heaven*, p. 100.

Chapter 7—Grace in the Midst of Judgment?
Albert Camus, *The Fall*

Originally published as " 'The Fall' and the Faith," in *Christianity and Crisis* (September 30, 1957), pp. 123–126.

Quotations are from Camus, *The Fall* (New York: Vintage Books, 1957).

Chapter 8—Fragments in the Midst of Brokenness:
Alan Paton, *Too Late the Phalarope*

Not previously published, save for the first two pages that appeared as "Alan Paton: Warrior and Man of Grace," *Christianity and Crisis* (June 6, 1988), pp. 204–205. The issue also includes a number of powerful quotations from a variety of Paton's writings.

Quotations are from Paton, *Too Late the Phalarope* (London: Jonathan Cape, 1955). Page references are in the text.

Chapter 9—Affirmation in the Midst of Complaint:
C. S. Lewis, *Till We Have Faces*

Originally published in a longer version as "The Complaint Against the Gods," in *Union Seminary Quarterly Review*, New York (May 1957), pp. 98–104.

Quotations are from Lewis, *Till We Have Faces* (London: Geoffrey Bles, 1950).

Chapter 10—Sainthood in the Midst of Earthiness:
Frederick Buechner, *Brendan*

Originally published as "The Land of the Blessed," in *Christianity and Crisis* (May 22, 1989), pp. 170–172.

Quotations are from Buechner, *Brendan* (San Francisco: Harper & Row, 1987). Page references are in the text.

Chapter 11—Strength in the Midst of Pain:
Alice Walker, *The Color Purple*

Not previously published.

1. I here record my disappointment that I was unable to gain permission to quote from *The Color Purple* in this chapter. No paraphrase, however skillful, can begin to match Alice Walker's prose, and I hope (in a somewhat difficult exercise of turning the other cheek) that readers who nevertheless respond to my own chapter will not stop there but will go directly to *The Color Purple* itself—a hope I naturally attach as well to all the other books dealt with here.

Chapter 12—Love in the Midst of Horror:
George Dennison, *Luisa Domic*

Originally published as "Wonders of Music and Love," in *Christianity and Crisis* (May 6, 1986), pp. 164–166.

Quotations are from Dennison, *Luisa Domic* (San Francisco: Harper & Row, 1985).

Chapter 13—Fantasy in the Midst of "Reality":
Ursula LeGuin, *Always Coming Home*

Originally published in a shorter version as "Middle Earth and the People of Kesh," in *Christianity and Crisis* (May 19, 1987), pp. 187–190.

Quotations are from LeGuin, *Always Coming Home* (New York: Harper & Row, 1989).

The initial quotation from Kierkegaard is in *Concluding Unscientific Postscript* (Princeton, N.J.: Princeton University Press, 1944), p. 554. The quotation from T. S. Eliot's "Little Gidding" is in *Four Quartets* (New York: Harcourt, Brace & Co., 1943), p. 39. References to Tolkien's trilogy are to Tolkien, *The Lord of the Rings*, Vol. I, *The Fellowship of the Ring;* Vol. II, *The Two Towers;* Vol. III, *The Return of the King* (London: George Allen & Unwin, Ltd., 1954–1955). The quotation from Robert Scholes is in *Structural Fabulation* (Notre Dame, Ind.: University of Notre Dame Press, 1975), p. 91.